Dear Reader,

The book you are holding came about in a rather different way to most others. It was funded directly by readers through a new website: Unbound. Unbound is the creation of three writers. We started the company because we believed there had to be a better deal for both writers and readers. On the Unbound website, authors share the ideas for the books they want to write directly with readers. If enough of you support the book by pledging for it in advance, we produce a beautifully bound special subscribers' edition and distribute a regular edition and e-book wherever books are sold, in shops and online.

This new way of publishing is actually a very old idea (Samuel Johnson funded his dictionary this way). We're just using the internet to build each writer a network of patrons. At the back of this book, you'll find the names of all the people who made it happen.

Publishing in this way means readers are no longer just passive consumers of the books they buy, and authors are free to write the books they really want. They get a much fairer return too – half the profits their books generate, rather than a tiny percentage of the cover price.

If you're not yet a subscriber, we hope that you'll want to join our publishing revolution and have your name listed in one of our books in the future. To get you started, here is a £5 discount on your first pledge. Just visit unbound.com, make your pledge and type **almanac5** in the promo code box when you check out.

Thank you for your support,

Dan, Justin and John
Founders, Unbound

THE
ALMANAC
2018

LIA LEENDERTZ

With illustrations by Emma Dibben

Unbound

This edition first published in 2017

Unbound
6th Floor Mutual House, 70 Conduit Street, London W1S 2GF
www.unbound.com

Illustrations © Emma Dibben, 2017

Shakkarpare and Thandai recipes, pp.51–52 © Ishita DasGupta
Atayef stuffed with walnuts recipe, pp.109–110 © Nisrin Abuorf
Curry goat recipe, p.148 © Natasha Miles

Book designed by Matt Cox at Newman+Eastwood

A CIP record for this book is available from the British Library

ISBN 978-1-78352-404-4 (trade hbk)
ISBN 978-1-78352-405-1 (ebook)
ISBN 978-1-78352-406-8 (limited edition)

Printed in Great Britain by Clays Ltd, St Ives Plc

9

For Lyssa, on the other side of the world, where the sun is also sinking down, and the moon slowly rising...
x

With special thanks to Hartley Botanic, a patron of this book

HARTLEY BOTANIC

NULLI SECUNDUS

HANDMADE WITH PRIDE SINCE 1938

CONTENTS

January

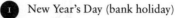

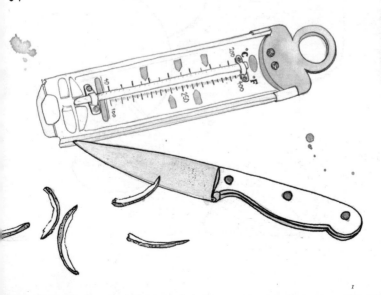

January is named after the Latin for door, *ianua*, being the opening onto the year. Neatly, doors feature heavily in New Year's celebrations. Traditionally, doors were flung open at midnight to let the old year out, saucepans banging to scare it away. The first person through your door after midnight sets the tone for the rest of your year: ideally your 'first footer' should be a tall, dark-haired man, bringing coal (for warmth), salt or money (riches), or bread and wine (plenty). Take nothing out of the door on New Year's Day, not even last night's bottles.

In January we often only step out through the door ourselves after ten minutes of dedicated cladding with wool and Gore-Tex, as the wind is keen and cutting, circling unscarfed necks and needling into the foolish gaps between tops and bottoms. Although midwinter falls in December, the warmth trapped in the land and the sea creates a lag, and the full chill of our tilt away from the sun and towards cold, dark space is only felt now.

But it is still worth getting out. The countryside has a bare beauty, all bones and hazes of purple and ochre in the low winter light, every last shred of green leaf having finally dropped. And once chilled to the bone, there will be log fires and marmalade-making and cosy puddings, back behind your own firmly closed front door.

THE SKY

Moon phases

Full moon – 2nd January

3rd quarter – 8th January

New moon – 17th January

1st quarter – 24th January

Full moon – 31st January

In the night sky this month

1st	Supermoon. The moon will be particularly close to the earth for this full moon and so may appear larger and brighter than normal.
3rd & 4th	The Quadrantid meteor shower, with up to 70 bluish and yellowish meteors per hour. Unfortunately this year it coincides with a full moon so may be hard to see.
7th	Mars and Jupiter in conjunction for several weeks, but closest tonight, visible before dawn in the southern sky.
9th	Venus changes from being a morning planet to an evening planet, but it will be lost in the glare of the sun for several weeks.
11th	Look out for a close approach of the crescent moon with Jupiter tonight, before dawn in the southern sky.

Constellation of the month – Orion

Orion is one of the most recognisable constellations, and beautifully visible in the winter sky. Look directly south at 10 p.m. in mid-January and it is around halfway between the horizon and the zenith, but it should not be hard to find at other times. Orion contains two of the ten brightest stars in the sky: Betelgeuse, a red supergiant in its top left-hand corner; and Rigel, a blue-white supergiant. When the sky is dark and clear, you will see a fuzzy 'star' a little below Orion's belt. This is the great Orion Nebula, the nearest region of massive star formation to earth, and hence one of the most studied objects in the sky.

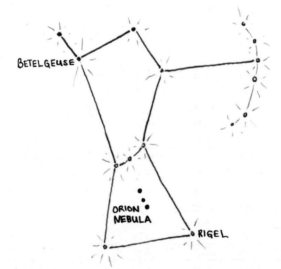

Moon rise and set

	London		Glasgow		
	Rise	Set	Rise	Set	
1st	15.49	06.59	15.45	07.38	full moon
2nd	16.55	08.05	16.51	08.44	
3rd	18.09	09.00	18.08	09.36	
4th	19.27	09.44	19.30	10.16	
5th	20.45	10.19	20.52	10.47	
6th	22.01	10.48	22.13	11.12	
7th	23.13	11.14	23.30	11.33	
8th	–	11.37	–	11.53	3rd quarter
9th	00.24	12.00	00.44	12.11	
10th	01.31	12.23	01.56	12.31	
11th	02.37	12.48	03.06	12.53	
12th	03.41	13.16	04.13	13.17	
13th	04.43	13.49	05.18	13.47	
14th	05.41	14.27	06.18	14.23	
15th	06.34	15.11	07.13	15.07	
16th	07.21	16.02	08.00	15.58	
17th	08.03	16.59	08.39	16.57	new moon
18th	08.38	18.00	09.12	18.01	
19th	09.08	19.04	09.39	19.08	
20th	09.35	20.10	10.02	20.18	
21st	09.59	21.17	10.22	21.30	
22nd	10.22	22.26	10.41	22.43	
23rd	10.45	23.37	11.00	23.58	
24th	11.08	–	11.20	–	1st quarter
25th	11.35	00.50	11.42	01.15	
26th	12.06	02.04	12.09	02.34	
27th	12.44	03.20	12.43	03.54	
28th	13.31	04.34	13.28	05.11	
29th	14.29	05.43	14.25	06.22	
30th	15.39	06.43	15.36	07.21	
31st	16.55	07.32	16.54	08.07	full moon

WEATHER

This is one of the two coldest months and the month in which we are most likely to see snow – 'as the day lengthens, so the cold strengthens'. In the north and Scotland, polar lows can move in, frequently bringing snow and blizzards. Low temperatures elsewhere are mitigated by proximity to the sea: the coldest areas are the mountains of Wales and northern England, as well as inland Scotland; the warmest and most likely to escape snow and ice are the south-western coasts. There is likely to be frost and fog throughout the country. Rain is very likely, and this is one of the two wettest months of the year.

Average temperatures (°C):	London 5, Glasgow 3
Average sunshine hours per day:	London 1, Glasgow 1
Average days rainfall:	London 19, Glasgow 25
Average rainfall total (mm):	London 55, Glasgow 130

Day length
During the course of January, day length increases by:

1 hour and 12 minutes, to 9 hours and 7 minutes (London)

1 hour and 29 minutes, to 8 hours and 35 minutes (Glasgow)

Sunrise and set

	London		Glasgow	
	Rise	Set	Rise	Set
1st	08.06	16.02	08.47	15.54
2nd	08.06	16.03	08.47	15.55
3rd	08.06	16.04	08.47	15.57
4th	08.06	16.06	08.46	15.58
5th	08.05	16.07	08.46	15.58
6th	08.05	16.08	08.45	16.01
7th	08.05	16.09	08.45	16.02
8th	08.04	16.11	08.44	16.04
9th	08.04	16.12	08.43	16.05
10th	08.03	16.13	08.42	16.07
11th	08.02	16.15	08.42	16.09
12th	08.02	16.15	08.41	16.10
13th	08.01	16.18	08.40	16.12
14th	08.00	16.19	08.39	16.14
15th	08.00	16.21	08.37	16.16
16th	07.59	16.22	08.36	16.18
17th	07.58	16.24	08.34	16.21
18th	07.57	16.26	08.34	16.21
19th	07.56	16.27	08.33	16.23
20th	07.55	16.29	08.31	16.25
21st	07.54	16.30	08.30	16.27
22nd	07.53	16.32	08.28	16.29
23rd	07.51	16.34	08.27	16.31
24th	07.50	16.36	08.25	16.34
25th	07.49	16.37	08.24	16.36
26th	07.48	16.39	08.22	16.38
27th	07.46	16.41	08.20	16.40
28th	07.45	16.43	08.19	16.42
29th	07.43	16.44	08.17	16.44
30th	07.42	16.46	08.15	16.46
31st	07.40	16.48	08.13	16.48

THE SEA

Average sea temperature

Orkney:	7.8°C
Scarborough:	7.3°C
Blackpool:	7.4°C
Brighton:	9.2°C
Penzance:	10.4°C

Spring and neap tides

The spring tide is the most extreme tide of the month, with the highest rises and falls, and the neap tide is the least extreme, with the smallest. Exact timings vary around the coast, but expect each around the following dates:

Spring tides:	3rd–4th and 18th–19th
Neap tides:	9th–10th and 25th–26th

Perigean tide

This month sees a relatively rare perigean spring tide, a particularly high tide caused by an alignment of moon and sun, coinciding with the moon being the closest it will swing towards the earth this month, on the 3rd–4th. To understand a perigean spring tide you need first to know your spring and neap tides. A spring tide occurs twice each month – a day or so after the moon is full and when it is new. At these moments, the earth, moon and sun have been almost perfectly aligned. The gravitational forces that the sun and moon exert on the earth's body of water have combined, leading to a particularly high high tide and a particularly low low tide. The day or so's delay is simply the time it takes for the pull to shift this huge body of water. When the moon is at its first quarter or third quarter it is at right angles to the line formed between the sun and earth, and therefore the sun and moon are pulling against each other. This results in much less dramatic tides with smaller rises and smaller falls: neap tides.

But there is a further factor at play: the elliptical orbit of the moon. The distance between the moon and the earth varies from 406,700 miles away to 356,500 miles away, and the closer it gets, the stronger the pull. The perigee is the moment the moon is closest to the earth each month, and this, of course, creates its own surge. Every month at some point the moon will move to its closest and furthest away, but it is only when the moon is at its closest and full that we get a supermoon, officially called a perigee full moon. This will happen this month on the 2nd, and within a day or two the pull on the earth's water will create a particularly extreme tide, with high tides raised by up to 25 per cent, and low tides dropping much further than usual too. This creates a flood risk of course, particularly during bad weather. The low tide is a good time to go fossil hunting for newly uncovered finds, or to beachcomb for interesting flotsam.

THE GARDEN

Planting by the moon

Full moon to 3rd quarter: 2nd–8th. Harvest crops for immediate eating. Harvest fruit.

3rd quarter to new moon: 8th–17th. Prune. Harvest for storage. Fertilise and mulch the soil.

New moon to 1st quarter: 17th–24th. Sow crops that develop below ground. Dig the soil.

1st quarter to full moon: 24th–31st. Sow crops that develop above ground. Plant seedlings and young plants.

Jobs in the garden
- Prune fruit trees and grape vines, to bring them back into shape.
- Force rhubarb clumps by covering them with a terracotta forcer or an upturned dustbin.
- Buy and chit (sprout on the windowsill) seed potatoes: the early bird gets the quirkiest varieties.

Glut of the month – swede
Brilliantly hardy, it grows sweeter and more complex the more winter throws at it.
- Bashed neeps: cube and boil until tender then mash with a near-excessive amount of butter, plenty of freshly ground black pepper, and salt. Serve with tatties and haggis at Burns Night on the 25th.
- Cornish pasties: sturdy shortcrust pastry (use strong white flour), beef skirt, waxy potatoes, swede and onion. Chop everything to the same size and bake for 20 minutes in a hot oven then 20 minutes in a medium oven.
- Swede with sausages and gravy: sauté swede slices in plenty of butter until slightly caramelised, then add a little stock, simmer until tender and roughly mash. Mound onto plate and serve with gravy and sausages.

Garden task – plant an apple tree

The cool and still inertia of the January garden can be turned
to our advantage, most particularly when moving things that
would rather not be moved. A tree that has dropped its leaves
is in a state of deep sleep, and like gently lifting a baby from
car seat to cot, there is an opportunity to make the move
almost without a whimper, and certainly without a tantrum.
This is the time to plant bare-root trees, lifted from the
ground by canny nurserymen and transported with their roots
wrapped in hessian, cheaper and available in greater variety
than those grown in pots. Apples are often sold this way.
Choose your variety and then find one grown on a suitable
rootstock, which helps to determine the size to which the tree
will eventually grow.

When the tree arrives, unwrap the roots and soak them in
a bucket of water. Dig your hole, plant, backfill, firm down
with a foot and then stake against rocking winds. Once in
place, and despite the continuing cold, the roots will start to
tentatively explore their new surroundings, and by the time
the first bud unfurls, your tree roots will be all settled in and
drinking up moisture, ready to make the most of spring,
summer and autumn.

M27   M9   M26   MM106   M25

KITCHEN

In season
- **Kale, kohlrabi, leeks, cabbage, cauliflower, carrot** and **swede** are all still standing in the vegetable garden. Early varieties of purple sprouting broccoli start to produce this month.
- Some **apples** and **pears** are still good if they have been well stored, as are **beetroots, garlic, onions, parsnips** and **squash**.
- There is lots of wonderful imported citrus around, and this month **blood oranges** join in. There are also lots of imported **pineapples, kiwis, passion fruits** and **pomegranates**.
- **Truffles** – black truffles are still arriving from Italy.
- **Hare, woodcock, pheasant** and **venison** are available from some butchers. **Duck** and **goose** are in season until the end of the month.

Ingredient of the month – Seville oranges
Early in the month the Seville oranges arrive, a brief but glowing respite from the gloom. Bitter and thick-skinned, zesty and complex, they are far closer to their sour Chinese ancestors than are sweet citruses. Almost the entire Mediterranean's crop is grown to be shipped to Britain, where in steaming kitchens over cups of tea and hours of Radio 4 it is transformed into bittersweet, golden orange marmalade to be spread onto thick toast. Buy them as soon as you see them and use them within the week: they are unwaxed and won't last. Jane Grigson's recipe uses 3 ¼ l water, 1 ½ kg oranges and 3 kg granulated sugar. Boil the oranges whole in the water for an hour and a half. Cool, halve, scoop out innards, and place them into a muslin, then squeeze this into the liquor before dropping it in with the chopped peel and the sugar. Bring slowly to the boil, stirring, then boil hard until a jam thermometer shows 105°C.

FESTIVITIES

Wassailing and Tu BiShvat: celebrating trees

January offers two festivities that celebrate trees and their crops. Both act as a reminder that summer and bounty will come again, and mark the start of the growing year, however unlikely that feels right now. Both also provide a perfect excuse to eat and drink by requiring the consumption of the crops they are celebrating, albeit in preserved form, as cider or as dried fruits.

Wassailing is an ancient custom of cider-producing regions of England, in which the wassail king or queen hangs pieces of cider-soaked toast in the branches of the most prominent or the oldest tree in an orchard, wassail songs are sung, cider is poured onto the roots, and favourable spirits are enticed towards the tree. 'Wassail' is also the name of the drink drunk on the day, and made by warming cider and apple juice with spices, sugar, oranges and lemons, and a dash of cider brandy. Finally, shots are fired through the branches, pots and pans are banged, and the evil spirits are warded off. A good harvest is hence guaranteed.

Tu BiShvat is a Jewish holiday that falls on the 15th day of the Hebrew month of Shevat, which this year means 31st January. It is also called Rosh Hashanah La'Ilanot, which translates as 'New Year of the Trees', and it has become a day of mass tree-planting in Israel. This moment marks the revival of the growing year after winter, and is the day from which the ages of trees are calculated to determine tithes. It is customary to eat dried tree fruits and nuts, or to make a feast featuring the seven species described in the Bible as being abundant in the land of Israel: wheat, barley, grapes, figs, pomegranates, olives and dates.

RECIPES

Date, apricot and pecan sticky toffee pudding

Sticky toffee pudding: warm, comforting and packed with chopped dates. The addition of a couple more of the crops of the Middle East does it no harm at all.

Ingredients

For the sauce

115 g butter

75 g golden caster sugar

40 g dark muscovado sugar

140 ml double cream

For the pudding

175 g Medjool dates, stoned and chopped small

50 g dried apricots, chopped small

300 ml boiling water

1 tsp bicarbonate of soda

50 g butter, softened

80 g golden caster sugar

80 g dark muscovado sugar

2 eggs, beaten

175 g plain white flour

1 tsp baking powder

Pinch of ground cloves

75 g pecans, roughly chopped

Method

Preheat your oven to 180°C and butter a baking dish 24 cm x 24 cm. Make the sauce by putting all of the ingredients in a saucepan together with a pinch of salt, heating slowly until they combine, and then boiling for a few minutes until the sauce thickens. Pour half of the sauce into the base of the dish and refrigerate while you make the pudding mix.

Put dates, apricots and bicarbonate of soda into a bowl and pour on the boiling water. Leave to soak and soften while you make the rest of the pudding. Cream the butter and sugar and then beat in the eggs one at a time. Stir in flour, baking powder and cloves, the fruit and its water, and the pecans. Stir well. Pour the batter onto the top of the sauce in the baking dish and bake for around 30 minutes, then remove from the oven, tip on the rest of the sauce, and grill under a medium grill until the sauce bubbles. Serve with ice cream or cream.

NATURE

Look out for:
- The first shoots of bulbs, proving that the season is turning under our feet.
- Hazel tree catkins start to appear. These are the hazel's male sexual organs and will disperse pollen while the tree is bare and there are no leaves to hinder it. Look also for the tiny, red female flowers on the stems, ready to catch it.
- Hellebores, which are called Christmas roses but rarely do anything at Christmas, start to flower now. Float a couple of flowers in a bowl of water to appreciate their intricacies.

Migrations

The winter thrushes: fieldfares and redwings.

These birds migrated to the UK from their northern European breeding grounds in September and October, searching for milder weather and more abundant food, but January often sees a micro-migration as cold weather drives them into towns and gardens. Normally they spend their days in arable fields and scrub and at the edges of woodlands, always travelling as a flock. But when the going gets cold, you may suddenly spot ten or twelve unfamiliar birds in a garden tree or picking over your cotoneaster. Fieldfares are large birds, the size of a blackbird, with a white underwing. Redwings are smaller, with an overall reddish-brown appearance and a red underwing. They like berries and love apples, so throw one onto the lawn when you are out feeding the rest of the birds.

Tracks in snow

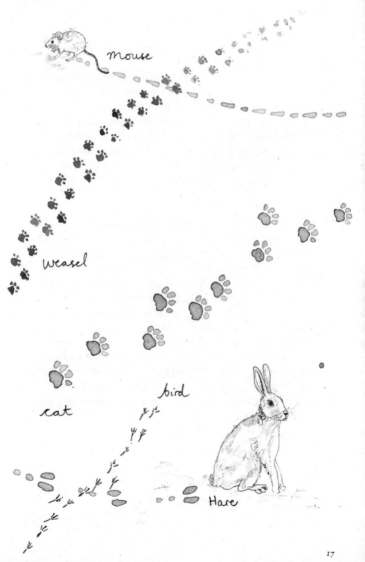

mouse

weasel

cat

bird

Hare

February

- **1** Imbolc (pagan celebration)
- **1** St Brigid's/St Bride's Day
- **2** Candlemas
- **13** Shrove Tuesday (Pancake Day)
- **14** Ash Wednesday, the beginning of Lent
- **14** St Valentine's Day
- **16** Chinese New Year, year of the Earth Dog begins

February is an ascetic little month. Cold, short and dark, many of its rituals – Imbolc, Candlemas, Lent – revolve around absence, purging and fasting. Its birthstone, amethyst, symbolises piety and humility. Even the name February comes from *februum*, Latin for purification, the root – *februo* – meaning 'I purify by sacrifice'. Fun old February. Because of its short length it is the only month that can pass without a full moon, and this year it does exactly this, so even the long nights are not lit up by the sparkling full winter moon. In all of this it can feel like a month of self-denial and of suspension of activity, a time to tuck up indoors and wait for warmer days, a pause for contemplation before the hustle and renewal of the next few months.

But look and you will see sure signs that nothing stands still, even – or perhaps especially – in February. In the far north of the country the day lengthens by a full two hours by the end of the month, and everywhere there are little signs of life returning, unable to resist the turning of the year even when breath is cloudy and ground solid. And as light returns so does the urge to sow and to grow, to start off the year's cycles, and to engage with the still-weak but strengthening sun. The temptation to hibernate may still be strong, but by the end of the month a spring-like hopefulness starts to win out.

THE SKY

Moon phases

3rd quarter – 7th February

New moon – 15th February

1st quarter – 23rd February

In the night sky this month

There will be no full moon this month, but there were two in January and will be two in March.

7th	Close approach of moon with Jupiter tonight, before dawn in southern sky.
9th	Close approach of moon with Mars tonight, before dawn in southern sky.

Constellation of the month – Canis Major

Follow the line of Orion's belt from the furthest right star
to the furthest left star and then beyond, and you will reach
Sirius, the Dog Star, the brightest star in the sky. It lies in the
constellation of Canis Major, the Great Dog, and is a major
constellation in the southern hemisphere, but from December
to March it can be seen in the northern hemisphere too, close
to the southern horizon. Together with the Little Dog, Canis
Minor, it chases Orion, the hunter, through the sky. Sirius is
in fact a binary star, or two stars orbiting around a common
point. The largest of the two, Sirius A, is twice the size of the
sun and 25 times as bright. Sirius's brightness is also down to
its proximity: at 8.6 light years away it is considered one of
our near neighbours.

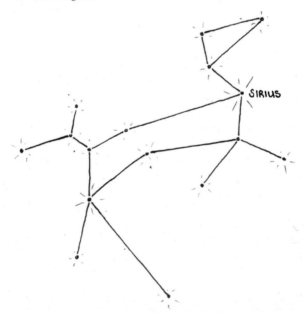

SIRIUS

Moon rise and set

	London		Glasgow		
	Rise	Set	Rise	Set	
1st	18.15	08.13	18.20	08.43	
2nd	19.34	08.46	19.44	09.12	
3rd	20.51	09.14	21.05	09.36	
4th	22.05	09.39	22.24	09.56	
5th	23.16	10.03	23.39	10.16	
6th	–	10.26	–	10.36	
7th	00.25	10.51	00.51	10.57	3rd quarter
8th	01.30	11.18	02.01	11.21	
9th	02.34	11.50	03.08	11.49	
10th	03.33	12.26	04.10	12.22	
11th	04.28	13.08	05.07	13.03	
12th	05.18	13.56	05.56	13.52	
13th	06.01	14.51	06.39	14.48	
14th	06.39	15.51	07.14	15.50	
15th	07.11	16.54	07.43	16.58	new moon
16th	07.39	18.00	08.07	18.08	
17th	08.04	19.08	08.28	19.20	
18th	08.27	20.18	08.48	20.33	
19th	08.50	21.28	09.07	21.48	
20th	09.14	22.40	09.26	23.04	
21st	09.39	23.53	09.47	–	
22nd	10.07	–	10.12	00.21	
23rd	10.42	01.07	10.42	01.39	1st quarter
24th	11.23	02.19	11.21	02.55	
25th	12.15	03.28	12.11	04.06	
26th	13.17	04.29	13.13	05.08	
27th	14.28	05.22	14.27	05.58	
28th	15.45	06.05	15.48	06.38	

WEATHER

The lengthening of days creates a huge sense of hope this month, and we gain nearly two hours of daylight by the end of it. But warmth does not match light, and this can be one of the very coldest months – minimum temperatures are often even lower than January's. The North Atlantic reaches its lowest temperature, and so negates the ameliorating effects of the Gulf Stream. Meanwhile, frequent easterly winds rush in from Siberia and chill to the bone.

Average temperatures (°C):	London 7, Glasgow 4
Average sunshine hours per day:	London 2, Glasgow 3
Average days rainfall:	London 16, Glasgow 22
Average rainfall total (mm):	London 35, Glasgow 90

Day length

During the course of February, day length increases by:

1 hour and 40 minutes, to 10 hours and 50 minutes (London)
1 hour and 58 minutes, to 10 hours and 37 minutes (Glasgow)

Sunrise and set

	London		Glasgow	
	Rise	Set	Rise	Set
1st	07.39	16.50	08.11	16.50
2nd	07.37	16.52	08.10	16.53
3rd	07.36	16.53	08.08	16.55
4th	07.34	16.55	08.06	16.57
5th	07.33	16.57	08.04	16.59
6th	07.31	16.59	08.02	17.01
7th	07.29	17.01	08.00	17.04
8th	07.27	17.03	07.57	17.06
9th	07.26	17.04	07.55	17.08
10th	07.24	17.06	07.53	17.10
11th	07.22	17.08	07.51	17.12
12th	07.22	17.10	07.49	17.14
13th	07.18	17.12	07.47	17.17
14th	07.17	17.14	07.44	17.19
15th	07.15	17.15	07.42	17.21
16th	07.13	17.17	07.40	17.23
17th	07.11	17.19	07.38	17.25
18th	07.09	17.21	07.35	17.28
19th	07.07	17.23	07.33	17.30
20th	07.05	17.25	07.30	17.32
21st	07.03	17.26	07.28	17.34
22nd	07.01	17.28	07.26	17.36
23rd	06.59	17.30	07.23	17.38
24th	06.57	17.32	07.21	17.41
25th	06.54	17.34	07.18	17.43
26th	06.52	17.35	07.16	17.45
27th	06.50	17.37	07.14	17.47
28th	06.48	17.39	07.11	17.49

THE SEA

Average sea temperature

Orkney:	7.3°C
Scarborough:	6.9°C
Blackpool:	7.2°C
Brighton:	8.7°C
Penzance:	10°C

Spring and neap tides

The spring tide is the most extreme tide of the month, with the highest rises and falls, and the neap tide is the least extreme, with the smallest. Exact timings vary around the coast, but expect each around the following dates:

Spring tides:	1st–2nd and 16th–17th
Neap tides:	8th–9th and 24th–25th

THE GARDEN

Planting by the moon

> **Full moon to 3rd quarter: 1st–7th.** Harvest crops for immediate eating. Harvest fruit.

> **3rd quarter to new moon: 7th–15th.** Prune. Harvest for storage. Fertilise and mulch the soil.

> **New moon to 1st quarter: 15th–23rd.** Sow crops that develop below ground. Dig the soil.

> **1st quarter to full moon: 23rd–28th.** Sow crops that develop above ground. Plant seedlings and young plants.

Jobs in the garden

- Prune last year's growth on wisteria back to two or three buds from the main framework.
- Weed, mulch and cover vegetable beds with black polythene, to warm the soil ready for spring planting.
- Cut back grasses and perennials that have been left all winter, but pile them up loosely and leave them in the garden, in case the stems contain overwintering creatures.

Glut of the month – rhubarb

If you covered your rhubarb at the beginning of January, you will have deep-pink stems ready for pulling.

- For pretty pink pieces to eat with custard or ice cream, roast, don't stew. Cut stems into 5-cm sections and place in a roasting tin with a few spoonfuls of orange juice, some honey, and a piece of star anise. Roast on a low heat for about 20 minutes.
- To make a fool you will need to make a puree, so stew the stems with a splash of water and a spoonful of sugar, stirring all the time. Leave to cool, and then mix very loosely into whipped cream.
- Try rhubarb raw, thinly sliced, topped with a little brown sugar or honey. A good topping for plain yoghurt.

Garden task – sow chillies

The urge to sow is strong this month, as daylight hours increase in leaps and bounds and we keenly sniff out any hint of spring. But despite our bones convincing us otherwise, it is way too early in the most part: seeds sown into the cold ground will rot away, and tender plants sown indoors this early will grow leggy, drawn and weak long before they can safely be planted out.

Chillies are the exception. Get hold of the catalogue of a specialist seed nursery and fully indulge those spring-like urges here. They need an epic growing season, and move slowly and with a naturally bushy habit, so will grow perfectly well indoors until the weather adequately warms.

Start them off one or two seeds to a pot on a warm, sunny windowsill. There are a few tricks to success with a chilli. Pot it into a slightly larger pot before it really needs it: they grow in response to root roominess and will be content with smallness if their pot is small. You must also resist any temptation to pinch out the growing tip in order to make it bushier: this is always the point from which the first fruit is borne, and you will set first cropping back by weeks if you do – it is bushy enough. And, finally, they need to bask in warmth and protection from the elements all summer long, ideally in a greenhouse. You will be rewarded for your early start in fiery fruits all through late summer.

chilli seeds

KITCHEN

In season

- **Clams, cockles** and **mussels** are all in season until March.
- Enjoy the brief **blood orange** season while it lasts. There may be a few around next month, but this is the height of the season. Imported **kiwi fruits, passion fruits, pineapples** and **pomegranates** are also plentiful and at their best.
- **Leeks, kale** and **cabbages** are still going well outdoors, if starting to look a little battered, and beautiful **purple sprouting broccoli** is now coming thick and fast.
- **Black truffles** are still available.
- **Pears, apples, carrots, swede** and **parsnips** are still good from storage.
- This is the final month of the **venison** season.

Ingredient of the month – sheep's cheese

For thousands of years before we fell for the charms of cow's milk, sheep's milk was the staple. Sheep's breeding cycles are strongly directed by day length – they breed as day length shortens and lamb as day length lengthens – and so unlike cows and goats, they cannot be easily convinced to breed and to produce milk all year round. This means that there is a definite season to the production of sheep's cheese, and this is the start of it. Sheep's milk is particularly rich and has a greater concentration of solids than goats or cow's milk, making it brilliant for cheese-making. Its cheese is particularly rich and sweet.

It will take weeks or months for the first hard cheese of the season to be mature, and these will last through the non-milking months too, but soft, fresh ewe's curd cheeses can be found from specialist dairies from now until autumn only.

FESTIVITIES

Imbolc and Candlemas

Scratch the surface of many traditional celebrations, and you often find that they are amalgams of Christian and older feast days, often with thematic echoes. The beginning of February sees the old pagan and Gaelic celebration of Imbolc (pronounced 'imulk') on the 1st and the Christian feast day of Candlemas on the 2nd, with both connected to purity, cleansing and hope. They fall roughly halfway between the shortest day and the spring equinox. Imbolc has seen something of a revival recently among modern Wiccans and Neo-pagans, and it provides a good marker for stopping and taking notice that winter is waning.

Imbolc's ritual cleansing was a sort of agricultural preparation: peasants would carry burning torches across farmland to purify the land prior to new planting, and to symbolise the ever-increasing strength of the sun. The celebration marks a stirring into life after winter. The word Imbolc may derive from the Old Irish *imbolc*, meaning 'in the belly', or from *oimelc*, meaning 'ewe's milk', both references to the importance of the arrival of sheep's milk into the diet at this time of year.

Candlemas is the Christian festival of light and celebrates Jesus's life as a baby and the ritual purification of Mary 40 days after his birth. *Lumen ad revelationem gentium*: a light to lighten the darkness of the world, as goes the canticle traditionally sung at the beginning of the Candlemas service. There is a candlelit procession and candles are brought into church to be blessed. Snowdrops, natural symbols of hope and purity, have a tentative link to both festivals. They were once commonly known as Candlemas bells, and it was considered unlucky to bring them into the house before Candlemas. *Galanthus nivalis* is the snowdrop's Latin name, and *Galanthus* is derived from the Greek words *gala* (milk) and *anthos* (flower).

RECIPES

Pancakes

A cold, dark Tuesday after school, coats still dripping in the
hall. An unlikely moment for a feast. But suddenly there is
ritual at the kitchen table: triangles of lemon arranged on a
saucer, sugar poured into a bowl. The first pancake is always
terrible, wet and floppy from being poured when the pan was
not yet blisteringly hot. Soon heat and confidence are up, and
the pancakes arrive from stove to table with greater speed, but
never, ever fast enough.

Makes about 12 pancakes
Ingredients
100 g plain flour
Pinch of salt
2 eggs, lightly beaten
300 ml milk
Oil for frying
Lemon wedges and caster sugar to serve

Method
Thirty minutes before you want to start cooking, put the flour
and salt into a large bowl and make a well in the centre. Tip
the eggs and a little of the milk into the well and use a whisk
to slowly bring in a little of the flour at a time, adding more
milk as it thickens, until all milk and flour are combined.
Set aside. Put a frying pan on a high heat and add a little oil.
Swirl a ladle full of batter around the pan and let it cook until
bubbles push up from underneath. Loosen, flip and cook for
a minute or two on the other side. Either serve them as they
arrive or keep a pile warm in a low oven.

Breeds of sheep

east friesian

blackface

hebridian

suffolk

ryeland

leicester longwool

Whipped sheep's cheese and shards of seedy crackers

To help stave off the urge to sow seeds, cook with them instead. Celebrate Imbolc with young cheese whipped until spoonable, and homemade seed-encrusted crackers. Soft, fresh goat's cheese is perfect too if you can't find sheep's.

Serves 4, as a snack
Ingredients
For the crackers
200 g plain flour
½ tsp baking powder
1 tsp salt
50 g cold butter, cut into cubes
4 tbsp water
4 tbsp each of sunflower, pumpkin and fennel seeds
1 tbsp sea salt flakes
For the whipped cheese
250 g soft sheep's or goat's cheese
2 tbsp extra virgin olive oil
Freshly ground pepper

Method
To make the crackers, preheat your oven to 180°C/350°F/gas mark 4, then mix together the flour, baking powder and salt and then rub in the butter. Pour in the water and form into a dough, adding more water if required. Knead briefly, roll into a rectangle, and place on a piece of parchment on a baking tray. Brush all over with water and then scatter on the seeds before pressing them gently into the dough.

Scatter over the sea salt flakes and bake for 10–15 minutes until golden. Remove, cool, and break into shards to eat.

Whip the soft cheese, olive oil and pepper together with a whisk until it is fluffy and then spoon it onto the cracker shards.

NATURE

Look out for:
- Snowdrops, naturalised en masse in woodlands. Dig a small clump from the garden and pot in an old terracotta container to appreciate them up close.
- Winter aconites: tiny, golden and spirit-lifting on even the greyest days. The first primroses, too.
- Listen out for mistle and song thrushes singing for territories.
- Large flocks of winter-visiting birds can be seen in the estuaries.
- Siskins, unusual but beautiful visitors to the bird table.

Frog, toad and newt spawn
On warm days towards the end of the month, frogs, toads and newts flock to ponds for several-day-long mating sessions, filling ponds with spawn. Frogspawn is always borne in clumps in shallow water, while toad spawn is borne in long chains, draped over pond weed and plants in deeper water. Newt spawn is less obvious, borne individually and folded into a leaf. Don't be alarmed by the amount: yes, there are too many potential frogs for your pond to support, but laying spawn is such a high-risk game that huge numbers are produced to allow for the many inevitable losses to predators and frosts. Don't move frogspawn to other ponds or lift some out to grow on in a bucket or tank: your pond really is the best place. If you know of a pond that does not contain any spawn, it is most probably because it is not suitable for frogs, otherwise they would have found it. Leave them be, and enjoy watching them develop over the coming months.

March

1 Start of meteorological spring

1 St David's Day (Wales)

2 Holi, the Hindu 'Festival of Colours', celebrating the end of winter

5 St Piran's Day (Cornwall)

11 Mother's Day

17 St Patrick's Day (Northern Ireland)

19 St Patrick's Day local holiday (Northern Ireland)

20 Vernal equinox

20 Start of astronomical spring

20 Ostara (pagan celebration)

25 Lady Day

25 Palm Sunday

25 1 a.m. – Daylight saving begins; clocks go forward one hour

29 Maundy Thursday

30 Good Friday (bank holiday)

31 First day of Passover (Jewish holiday)

In blustery March, light finally wins out over darkness. The vernal equinox falls on the 20th, when day and night are of equal length, and the clocks go forward on the 25th, giving a sudden extra hour of light every evening. Spring feels irresistible now: summer-visiting birds begin to return, bumblebees are tentatively buzzing, the ground can be cultivated. Yellow is the colour of March: bright daffodils, winter aconites, primroses, lemon-toned brimstone butterflies and bright spring sunshine, at least in between the showers and the gales.

March was once a pivotal moment in the year. In the Roman calendar March, or Martius, was the first month, and in Britain 25th March – Lady Day – remained the beginning of the legal year until 1752; some old land tenancies still run from Lady Day to Lady Day. The month was named after Mars, the god of war and – less famously – the guardian of agriculture. March was considered the month when both farming and warfare could begin, because no one wants to be out crusading in the snow. The Saxons called it Lentmonat, or lengthening month, because of the equinox and the noticeable lengthening of days, and this is the origin of the word Lent, which itself runs throughout March. Other Anglo-Saxon names for March included Hlydmonath, meaning stormy month, and Hraedmonath, meaning rugged month, both of which give a good flavour to the experience of being outdoors at the moment.

THE SKY

Moon phases

Full moon – 2nd March

3rd quarter – 9th March

New moon – 17th March

1st quarter – 24th March

Full moon – 31st March

In the night sky this month

7th	Close approach of moon with Jupiter tonight, visible in the south from about 1 a.m. They reach maximum height at 4.30 a.m.
11th	Close approach of moon with Saturn tonight, low in southern sky around 5 a.m.
31st	Second full moon of the month (blue moon).

Constellation of the month – Ursa Major

Ursa Major, the Great Bear, climbs to its spring position high in the sky this month, tail down, nose up. It is best known for the Plough or the Big Dipper, the asterism which forms its centre (and the tail and body of the bear). You can use pointer stars within the Big Dipper to locate the North Star, or Polaris. It was used by escaping slaves in southern USA to point the way to the free states in the north, hence the folk song 'Follow the Drinking Gourd', this being another name for the Big Dipper. The side of the 'bowl' part of the Big Dipper furthest from the 'handle' part comprises two stars, Merak at the base and Dubhe at the rim. Draw a line between these two and extend it about five times and you will reach Polaris. Polaris is not the brightest star in the sky, but it is the most important, as the axis of the earth is pointed almost directly at it, so it does not rise or set or move through the sky. The other stars rotate around it and you can use it to locate due north at any time of year.

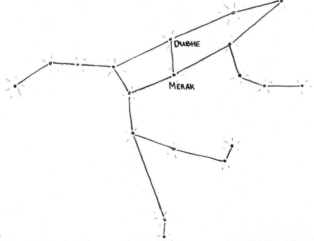

Moon rise and set

	London		Glasgow		
	Rise	Set	Rise	Set	
1st	17.05	06.41	17.12	07.10	
2nd	18.23	07.11	18.35	07.35	full moon
3rd	19.40	07.38	19.56	07.57	
4th	20.54	08.02	21.15	08.18	
5th	22.06	08.26	22.31	08.38	
6th	23.15	08.51	23.44	08.59	
7th	–	09.18	–	09.22	
8th	00.21	09.48	00.54	09.48	
9th	01.23	10.22	01.59	10.20	3rd quarter
10th	02.20	11.02	02.59	10.58	
11th	03.12	11.48	03.51	11.43	
12th	03.58	12.41	04.36	12.37	
13th	04.37	13.39	05.14	13.37	
14th	05.11	14.41	05.45	14.43	
15th	05.41	15.47	06.10	15.53	
16th	06.07	16.55	06.33	17.05	
17th	06.31	18.05	06.53	18.19	new moon
18th	06.54	19.16	07.12	19.35	
19th	07.18	20.29	07.31	20.52	
20th	07.42	21.43	07.52	22.11	
21st	08.10	22.58	08.16	23.30	
22nd	08.42	–	08.44	–	
23rd	09.21	00.11	09.19	00.47	
24th	10.09	01.21	10.05	01.59	1st quarter
25th	12.06	03.24	12.02	04.03	
26th	13.13	04.18	13.10	04.55	
27th	14.26	05.02	14.26	05.37	
28th	15.42	05.40	15.47	06.10	
29th	17.00	06.11	17.09	06.37	
30th	18.16	06.38	18.30	07.00	
31st	19.31	07.03	19.50	07.20	full moon

Moon map

1. Mare Frigoris
   Sea of Cold

2. Plato (Crater)

3. Mare Imbrium
   Sea of Rains

4. Aristarchus (Crater)

5. Archemedes (Crater)

6. Mare Serenitatis
   Sea of Serenity

7. Mare Crisium
   Sea of Storms

8. Eratosthenes (Crater)

9. Oceanus Procellarum
   Ocean of Storms

10. Copernicus (Crater)

11. Mare Tranquillitatis
    Sea of Tranquility

12. Ptolemaeus (Crater)

13. Mare Foecunditatis
    Sea of Fertility

14. Mare Nubium
    Sea of Clouds

15. Mare Nectaris
    Sea of Nectar

16. Mare Humorum
    Sea of Moisture

17. Schickard (Crater)

18. Tycho (Crater)

M

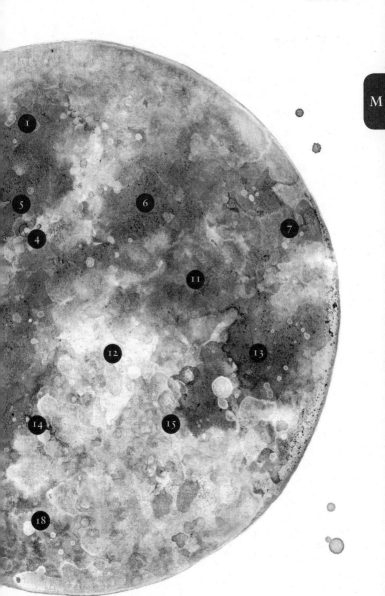

WEATHER

The saying that March 'comes in like a lion and goes out like a lamb' almost never proves true, but it is indicative of the turbulence of the weather at this moment in the year, and its potential to turn mild and spring-like, then chilly and blustery in quick succession. The beginning of March marks the start of meteorological spring, and March also contains the spring equinox, when day and night are the same length. But despite encouraging and spring-like increases of light, March can be a very cold month, and it is just as likely to snow this month as it was in February. Significant plant growth only takes place above 6°C, and the temperature will waver above and below that, so that by the end of this month spring will definitely have sprung green and keen in some parts of the country, while others will still look and feel wintry.

Average temperatures (°C):	London 9, Glasgow 4
Average sunshine hours per day:	London 4, Glasgow 3
Average days rainfall:	London 16, Glasgow 22
Average rainfall total (mm):	London 35, Glasgow 90

Day length

During the course of March, day length increases by:

1 hour and 29 minutes, to 12 hours and 25 minutes (London)
2 hours and 20 minutes, to 13 hours and 2 minutes (Glasgow)

On the vernal equinox on the 20th, night and day are of the same length. It is one of only two days a year (the other being the autumnal equinox in September) when the sun rises precisely due east and sets due west.

Sunrise and set

	London		Glasgow	
	Rise	Set	Rise	Set
1st	06.46	17.41	07.09	17.51
2nd	06.44	17.42	07.06	17.53
3rd	06.42	17.44	07.04	17.55
4th	06.39	17.46	07.01	17.57
5th	06.37	17.48	06.58	18.00
6th	06.35	17.49	06.56	18.02
7th	06.33	17.51	06.53	18.04
8th	06.31	17.53	06.51	18.06
9th	06.28	17.55	06.48	18.08
10th	06.26	17.56	06.46	18.10
11th	06.24	17.58	06.43	18.12
12th	06.22	18.00	06.40	18.14
13th	06.19	18.01	06.38	18.16
14th	06.17	18.03	06.35	18.18
15th	06.15	18.05	06.33	18.20
16th	06.13	18.07	06.30	18.22
17th	06.10	18.08	06.27	18.24
18th	06.08	18.10	06.25	18.26
19th	06.06	18.12	06.22	18.29
20th	06.04	18.13	06.20	18.31
21st	06.01	18.15	06.17	18.33
22nd	05.59	18.17	06.14	18.35
23rd	05.57	18.18	06.12	18.37
24th	05.54	18.20	06.09	18.39
25th*	06.52	19.22	07.09	19.41
26th	06.50	19.24	07.04	19.43
27th	06.48	19.25	07.01	19.45
28th	06.45	19.27	06.59	19.47
29th	06.43	19.29	06.56	19.49
30th	06.41	19.30	06.53	19.51
31st	06.38	19.32	06.51	19.53

*Note: on the 25th this chart switches from Greenwich Mean Time to British Summer Time.

THE SEA

Average sea temperature

Orkney:	7.1°C
Scarborough:	6.8°C
Blackpool:	7.3°C
Brighton:	8.2°C
Penzance:	9.7°C

Spring and neap tides

The spring tide is the most extreme tide of the month, with the highest rises and falls, and the neap tide is the least extreme, with the smallest. Exact timings vary around the coast, but expect each around the following dates:

Spring tides:	3rd–4th and 18th–19th
Neap tides:	10th–11th and 25th–26th

Seabird colonies

If you are close to coastal cliffs, this is the month to watch seabird colonies reassemble, to enjoy the racket, and to dodge the deposits. Seabirds such as puffins, northern gannets, Manx shearwaters, shags, kittiwakes and storm petrels come in to shore to nest and raise their young.

kittiwake

THE GARDEN

Planting by the moon

Full moon to 3rd quarter: 2nd–9th. Harvest crops for immediate eating. Harvest fruit.

3rd quarter to new moon: 9th–17th. Prune. Harvest for storage. Fertilise and mulch the soil.

New moon to 1st quarter: 17th–24th. Sow crops that develop below ground. Dig the soil.

1st quarter to full moon: 24th–31st. Sow crops that develop above ground. Plant seedlings and young plants.

Jobs in the garden
- Start sowing hardier vegetable seeds outdoors: peas, broad beans, spinach and parsnips can all be direct-sown. Make a nursery bed and thickly sow leeks to be spaced out later. Plant out potatoes at the end of the month.
- In the greenhouse sow cucumbers, aubergines, Florence fennel, Brussels sprouts, sprouting broccoli, cabbages, and, towards the end of the month, start to sow tomatoes.
- Big clumps of snowdrops can be lifted, split and replanted now that the flowers are passed, to spread them about. Buy new snowdrops now while they are 'in the green', as they establish best at this stage.

Glut of the month – leeks
In the 'hungry gap' between last year's stored produce running out and this year's starting up, leeks are one of the few stalwarts still standing on the vegetable plot.
- Slice leeks in half, wash thoroughly, then cut up and slow-cook in plenty of butter and a pinch of salt, covered, until the leeks are meltingly soft. Cook for a few more minutes uncovered. Top with a piece of poached fish or a fried egg.
- Poach young leeks (or large leeks sliced in half lengthways)

in salted water for 8–10 minutes until tender, drain and toss with extra virgin olive oil, a little cider vinegar, chopped capers and salt and pepper.

* Make Glamorgan sausages for St David's Day. Mix two slow-cooked leeks with crumbled Caerphilly cheese, a handful of breadcrumbs, chopped thyme and parsley, and two beaten eggs. Chill for half an hour in the fridge then form into short sausages, roll in breadcrumbs and fry.

Garden task – plant dahlias
The glamorous darlings of the late-summer garden, dahlias need to be started into growth now, and they are far easier than their exotic looks suggest. This is a good moment to buy tubers – the big, fleshy roots – and to pot them up in a greenhouse or on a cool indoor windowsill. It is possible to plant them straight outside if you wait until the weather is warmer, but slugs love them. Better to give dahlias a head start in an environment where you can fend off the molluscs, then plant them out when they are big and healthy.

Dahlias are as varied in form as they are in colour. Pompom types are neat and perfect balls of incurved petals; decorative types are big, bold and fully double; the petals of cactus types are pointed; waterlily types are flat flowers with gently curving petals. Choose a rough colour scheme and take one of each type for particularly satisfying bouquet mixing. 'Café au Lait' is a beautiful peachy and creamy decorative bloom, and looks particularly fine alongside pinky-purple 'American Dawn' and dark and brooding 'Summer Night'.

Take generous pots, half fill them with fresh compost, carefully lower in the delicate tuber and fill in around with compost, pressing down with fingers to fill in the air gaps. Water well and keep free of frost. You can plant them out in May and start picking in mid to late summer.

KITCHEN

M

In season

- **Swiss chard**, **spring onions** and **winter lettuces** all have new growth and are ready for harvesting now. The last of the **Brussels sprouts** can be picked. **Purple sprouting broccoli** and **rhubarb** are plentiful. This is the last month for **winter cabbages** and the first for **spring cabbages**.
- This is the last month for stored **cooking apples**. Stored **eating apples** and **pears** are generally over.
- **Oysters** and **mussels** are still in season but will soon be gone. **Halibut, cod, coley, dab, lemon sole** and other winter fish are still in season too.
- **Sheep's** and **goat's milk cheeses** are good now, made from the new fresh milk.

Ingredient of the month – mussels

The months with an 'R' in their name are when there is the most 'meat' on a mussel, before it spawns and turns lean in late spring when the sea warms. Have a good sniff when you buy them: they should smell fresh like the sea. Don't buy them too clean as they keep best with the 'beard' still attached. Store them in the fridge in newspaper and use within two days, cleaning the beards off with a paring knife and scrubbing the mussels under running water just before using. Combine finely chopped shallots and plenty of garlic with a couple of glasses of white wine in a big stock pot, bring to the boil and simmer for 5 minutes. Turn up the heat, drop in the mussels and cover for 5 minutes until all are open. Stir in a big handful of herbs and lots of butter, remove from the heat, and eat with good bread to soak up the juices.

FESTIVITIES

Holi

The colourful and chaotic festival of Holi is a Hindu celebration of the end of winter and the beginning of spring, and it coincides with the full moon that falls before the vernal equinox, this year on 2nd March. It originates in India but is celebrated by the Hindu population in Nepal and by the diaspora across the globe, including in Fiji, the Caribbean, Mauritius and, increasingly, Britain.

There are a number of legends associated with Holi. One concerns Prahlada, who was a devotee of Lord Vishnu against his father's wishes, and who, for this crime, was tricked into sitting on a pyre by his aunt Holika. When he miraculously survived the fire and his aunt burned, his father flew into a rage and smashed a pillar, at which Lord Vishnu appeared and killed the father. Another is the story of Lord Shiva and Kamadeva, the goddess of love, who tried to jolt Shiva out of his penance and meditation after the death of his wife Sati.

A fire is lit on the first day of Holi, symbolic of the fire that burned Holika and of the victory of good over evil and light over darkness, in echoes of Christian and pagan spring fire-based festivals Candlemas and Beltane. The urge to celebrate the returning of life and light seems universal. The fire's ashes are dabbed onto foreheads; the next day is Rangwali Holi, a carnival of colours, with bright-coloured powders and coloured water thrown freely at every passer-by. This is in celebration of Lord Krishna, who would apply pigments playfully to Radha and the other *gopis* (cowherds), this play becoming popular and part of tradition. The changing of the seasons being a time when many fall prey to colds and viruses, powdered medicinal plants were originally the source of the colours: turmeric, spring herbs, hibiscus flowers, beetroot and grapes. After the fun, there is visiting and sweet delicacies. *Bhang* or marijuana is often added to drinks during Holi, particularly celebrating Lord Shiva's triumph over evil.

RECIPES

Shakkarpare A recipe by Ishita DasGupta

During Holi, crisp fried foods and sweet things abound. *Shakkarpare*, originating from Maharashtra in central India, are flaky little pastries coated in sugar syrup that are eaten as a snack and go so well alongside *thandai*. If you don't have chapati flour, fine wholemeal flour may be substituted.

Serves 6–8
Ingredients
240 g *atta* (chapati flour),
2 tbsp ghee (at room temperature),
75–100 ml water
Ghee/oil for frying

For the syrup
150 g caster sugar or 100 g grated jaggery
125 ml water

Method

Place the *atta* into a mixing bowl, add the ghee and rub it through. Slowly add the water until it all comes together in a soft ball. It should not feel too wet or sticky. Cover the bowl and leave to rest for 20 minutes at room temperature. Roll the dough out to the thickness of a pound coin and cut into diamond shapes 4–5 cm in length and 2 cm wide.

Put the caster sugar and water into a saucepan and place over a medium heat. Do not stir but allow the sugar to dissolve. Once clear, the syrup is ready.

In a *karahi* or *wok*, pour enough oil or ghee until it is 1 cm deep and place over a moderately high heat. Add one of the pastry diamonds to test the oil – when it is hot enough it will foam and take 15–20 seconds for each side to turn golden. Remove and blot on a plate lined with kitchen roll. Once all the pastry diamonds have been fried, place into the warm syrup and stir through. Transfer to a bowl to cool. These are best eaten on the same day but will keep in an airtight container for a day or two.

Thandai A recipe by Ishita DasGupta

Thandai, meaning 'cooling', is a drink synonymous with Holi. Thickened with almond paste, scented with rose water and bursting with fennel and cardamom, it is sweet and comforting. Some people add bhang or marijuana to it for Holi.

Serves 4–6

Ingredients

75 g blanched almonds
1 tsp melon seeds
10 green cardamom – seeds only
1 ½ tsp fennel seeds
½ tsp black peppercorns
½ tsp coriander seeds
50–75 g caster sugar
750 ml whole milk
2 tbsp rose water

Method

Place the almonds and melon seeds in a bowl, with enough warm water to cover them and leave for two hours. In a shallow frying pan or *tawa*, toast the spices and set aside. Blend the nuts, seeds, toasted spices and sugar to a paste in a blender or pestle and mortar. Scoop the paste into a saucepan and add the milk and rose water. Bring up to the boil; remove immediately from the heat and leave to cool. Once cool, strain into a jug using a sieve or muslin and refrigerate until chilled.

M

NATURE

Look out for:
- The return of summer-visiting birds: wheatears and chiffchaffs are the first arrivals.
- Blackthorn in flower – note the spot for sloes in autumn.
- Mad March hares: this is the name given to female hares energetically resisting the advances of male hares, and while arable fields are still short this is a good time to spot them.
- Wood anemone, sweet violet, stinking hellebore and dog's mercury on the woodland floor.
- Skylarks and lapwings begin singing above arable fields, skylarks melodious and hovering high above, lapwings calling 'peewit' while tumbling almost to the ground and rising back up again.
- Fluffy goat-willow catkins, on plants growing in damp soil alongside rivers or lakes.
- The first butterfly of the year to emerge: the pale yellow or green brimstone.

Wild and naturalised daffodils
Our native daffodil *Narcissus pseudonarcissus* is pretty, pale and delicate, known as the Lent lily, and once widely and affectionately called the 'daffydowndilly'. Due to habitat loss it is not nearly as common as it once was, but clumps and drifts can still be found, tossing their heads in the March breezes, in fields and on verges down the western half of the country. The best place to see them is Gloucestershire's 'Golden Triangle', where a ten-mile footpath known as the Daffodil Way runs through woods, orchards and meadows. The Tenby daffodil, *Narcissus pseudonarcissus subsp. obvallaris*, is small and sturdy and a bolder yellow. It may have originated as a cultivated flower but it now grows wild across west Wales. Look out too for clumps of unusual daffodils flowering in Cornish verges. These may be remnants of heritage cultivars, once the stalwarts of the Cornish flower industry, but dumped along road edges during the Second World War when farmers had to turn their fields over to food production.

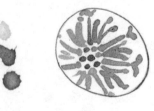

April

 Easter Sunday

 April Fools' Day

2 Easter Monday (local holiday in England, Wales, Northern Ireland, Guernsey, Jersey)

7 Last day of Passover (Jewish celebration)

11 Yom HaShoah (Holocaust Remembrance Day)

13 Isra and Mi'raj (Muslim celebration)

23 St George's Day (England)

The Romans named April Aprilis, possibly from the verb *aperire* (to open), and although no one quite knows why, it fits in well with the atmosphere of the month: buds bursting and windows being flung wide as warmth arrives, at least briefly, between showers. We are past the spring equinox now and life is tripping over itself to get going, to get on. The soft haze of lime-green tips over dark winter branches that appeared last month is filling out daily, and colourful garden flowers start to join the white blossom of blackthorn, damson and pear, filling the air with scent, luring in emerging bees in a frenzy of pollination.

The Anglo-Saxons called it Eosturmonath, the month of the goddess Ëostre, of whom little is known but much imagined, as there seems an irresistibly etymological link between Ëostre and Easter. The word Ëostre could point to oestrogen, to womanhood and the potential for pregnancy, to eggs and bunnies themselves. It also suggests the east, and the dawn, and hope. All conjecture, but it certainly fits well with this burgeoning and expectant month, full of promise.

THE SKY

Moon phases

3rd quarter – 8th April

New moon – 16th April

1st quarter – 22nd April

Full moon – 30th April

A

In the night sky this month

2nd	Conjunction of Mars and Saturn for several weeks, but at their closest tonight low in the southern dawn sky.
7th	Close approach of moon with Saturn tonight, low above the southern horizon before dawn.
17th	Close approach of moon with Venus tonight, low above the western horizon from about 8.30 p.m.; difficult to see as the moon is only a day old.
22nd & 23rd	Lyrid meteor shower, moon sets after midnight, leaving a good, dark sky for meteor-spotting.
30th	Close approach of moon with Jupiter tonight, highest at 1.46 a.m., 22 degrees above the southern horizon.

Constellation of the month – Hydra

This month the water snake, Hydra, can be seen rearing up from the horizon in the south-western sky when viewed around 11 p.m. It is a southern-hemisphere star, seen best south of the equator, but it can be spotted in the northern hemisphere between January and May and reaches its highest point in April. This is the largest of all the constellations, slithering a full 100 degrees across the sky. However, it has only one particularly bright star, Alphard, an orange giant with three times the mass of the sun; this is the star that appears on the Brazilian flag. Hydra is an adaptation of a Babylonian constellation, and so one of the earliest to have been plucked out of the sky.

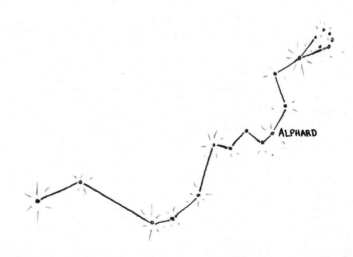

ALPHARD

Moon rise and set

	London		Glasgow		
	Rise	Set	Rise	Set	
1st	20.44	07.26	21.08	07.40	
2nd	21.56	07.51	22.23	08.00	
3rd	23.04	08.16	23.36	08.22	
4th	–	08.45	–	08.47	
5th	00.10	09.18	00.45	09.16	
6th	01.10	09.56	01.48	09.52	
7th	02.05	10.39	02.44	10.34	
8th	02.54	11.30	03.33	11.25	3rd quarter
9th	03.35	12.25	04.13	12.22	
10th	04.11	13.26	04.46	13.26	
11th	04.42	14.30	05.13	14.34	
12th	05.09	15.37	05.37	15.45	
13th	05.34	16.47	05.57	16.59	
14th	05.57	17.58	06.16	18.15	
15th	06.20	19.12	06.35	19.33	
16th	06.44	20.27	06.55	20.53	new moon
17th	07.11	21.44	07.18	22.14	
18th	07.42	23.00	07.44	23.35	
19th	08.19	–	08.18	–	
20th	09.04	00.13	09.00	00.51	
21st	01.20	09.59	09.54	01.59	
22nd	11.03	02.17	11.00	02.56	1st quarter
23rd	12.14	03.04	12.14	03.04	
24th	13.29	03.43	13.32	04.15	
25th	14.45	04.14	14.52	04.42	
26th	16.00	04.42	16.12	05.05	
27th	17.14	05.06	17.31	05.25	
28th	18.27	05.29	18.48	05.44	
29th	19.38	05.52	20.04	06.03	
30th	20.48	06.17	21.18	06.24	full moon

Lyrid meteor showers, and observing meteors

This month sees the Lyrid meteor shower. Meteors might be seen at any time from the 16th to the 25th, but are most likely to come in a burst at dawn on the 22nd. The Lyrids radiate from the constellation Lyra, but will appear all over the sky. You can hope to see up to 20 meteors an hour at the shower's peak, and about a quarter of the Lyrid's meteors have persistent trains: ionised gas trails that glow for a few seconds after they first streak across the sky. Meteors appear when the earth travels through the debris left by a comet, in this case Comet Thatcher, which last came close in 1861. Each meteor seen streaking through the sky is likely to have been caused by a tiny fragment of between 1 mm and 1 cm in diameter, burning up in the earth's atmosphere. Just before dawn is always the best time to see meteor showers. At dawn the planet rotates so that our position upon it is the leading point as we hurtle through space, sweeping up comet particles.

WEATHER

April has a reputation for showers, but it is actually one of
the drier months. It is possible that we just notice the showers
more because of their nature: April days can often start warm
and sunny but then the few wisps of cloud build into towering
cumulonimbus rain clouds, drop their load, then disperse into
blue sky again. This pattern occurs when there is a contrast
between warm surface air and colder air higher up, and
this often happens in April, when the sun warms the earth
but cool northerly or north-westerly air is blowing in from
Greenland or the Arctic. Despite balmy potential, sharp frosts
are common this month, and there can still be heavy snow in
the hills.

Average temperatures (°C):	London 11, Glasgow 11
Average sunshine hours per day:	London 5, Glasgow 5
Average days rainfall:	London 16, Glasgow 22
Average rainfall total (mm):	London 43, Glasgow 50

Day length
During the course of April, day length increases by:

1 hour and 50 minutes, to 14 hours and 47 minutes (London)
2 hours and 11 minutes, to 15 hours and 17 minutes (Glasgow)

Sunrise and set

	London		Glasgow	
	Rise	Set	Rise	Set
1st	06.36	19.34	06.48	19.55
2nd	06.34	19.35	06.46	19.57
3rd	06.32	19.37	06.43	19.59
4th	06.29	19.39	06.40	20.01
5th	06.27	19.40	06.38	20.03
6th	06.25	19.42	06.35	20.05
7th	06.23	19.44	06.33	20.07
8th	06.21	19.45	06.30	20.09
9th	06.18	19.47	06.27	20.11
10th	06.16	19.49	06.25	20.13
11th	06.14	19.50	06.22	20.15
12th	06.12	19.52	06.20	20.17
13th	06.10	19.54	06.17	20.19
14th	06.07	19.55	06.15	20.21
15th	06.05	19.57	06.12	20.23
16th	06.03	19.59	06.10	20.25
17th	06.01	20.00	06.07	20.27
18th	05.59	20.02	06.05	20.28
19th	05.57	20.04	06.02	20.31
20th	05.55	20.05	06.00	20.33
21st	05.53	20.07	05.57	20.35
22nd	05.50	20.09	05.55	20.37
23rd	05.48	20.10	05.53	20.39
24th	05.46	20.12	05.50	20.42
25th	05.44	20.14	05.48	20.44
26th	05.42	20.15	05.45	20.46
27th	05.40	20.17	05.43	20.48
28th	05.38	20.19	05.41	20.50
29th	05.36	20.20	05.38	20.52
30th	05.35	20.22	05.36	20.54

THE SEA

Average sea temperature

Orkney:	7.8°C
Scarborough:	8.1°C
Blackpool:	8.9°C
Brighton:	9.6°C
Penzance:	10.6°C

Spring and neap tides

The spring tide is the most extreme tide of the month, with the highest rises and falls, and the neap tide is the least extreme, with the smallest. Exact timings vary around the coast, but expect each around the following dates:

Spring tides:	1st–2nd and 17th–18th
Neap tides:	9th–10th and 23rd–24th

THE GARDEN

Planting by the moon

> **Full moon to 3rd quarter: 1st–8th.** Harvest crops for immediate eating. Harvest fruit.

> **3rd quarter to new moon: 8th–16th.** Prune. Harvest for storage. Fertilise and mulch the soil.

> **New moon to 1st quarter: 16th–22nd.** Sow crops that develop below ground. Dig the soil.

> **1st quarter to full moon: 22nd–30th.** Sow crops that develop above ground. Plant seedlings and young plants.

Jobs in the garden
- Plant out your potatoes into trenches, with enough space between rows to earth them up – cover the green stems – once they start to grow. Plant a few earlies into big pots too, for a quicker crop.
- Start growing tomatoes, aubergines, courgettes and winter squashes in pots on the windowsill or in a greenhouse.
- Start cutting your lawn, and re-seed any bare patches. You will soon have it looking welcoming again.

Glut of the month – sorrel

Sorrel is a perennial plant that pops up early in the year, with delicious lemony but savoury leaves. They collapse dramatically, like spinach, so pick and cook plenty. Wash sorrel well and remove the central stalk by pulling it back on itself before cooking.

- Put a third of a pack of butter in a pan, drop in big handfuls of sorrel leaves and tip in just-boiled and drained potatoes. Mix until the butter melts and the sorrel wilts into a mushy and sharp sauce, of sorts.
- Sorrel's acidity is good with oily salmon. Cook handfuls of washed sorrel in a little water until it collapses, then

squeeze out excess liquid. Process with a splash of cream and two egg yolks, then warm in a saucepan until the sauce thickens. Pour over baked salmon.

- Use sorrel in a frittata. Cook and drain it first, then mix loosely into beaten eggs, perhaps with some young peas, and cook.

Garden task – start a hardy annual cut-flower bed

There are few greater harvests than cut flowers, few more luxurious returns for a bit of digging and sowing: vases of flowers all summer long and bunches to hand magnanimously out to friends, too. Hardy annuals are particularly dependable and abundant, and should be the core of your patch. They are the simplest of the cut flowers to grow, as they can be started off by sowing direct into the ground. A word of warning before you do this: this time of year is wildly unpredictable and you should hold off if the weather or the soil is particularly cold. Pre-warm the soil by covering with black or clear plastic, or cover your newly sown rows with cloches. Either or both will give your seedlings a gentler start during this unsettled meteorological spell.

Some of the best hardy annuals to try: calendula, cornflower, larkspur, *Ammi majus*, nigella, *Cerinthe*, *Molucella* and *Griffithii*. These will give you a good variety of colour and shape, and a mix of showy performers and background fillers; even if you grow nothing else, you will have many joyous bunches. Work your soil until it is fine and crumbly, make a drill and crumble compost along it, then finely sow the seeds all along the drill; cover, water and label. If you have space in a greenhouse, sow a few seeds into seed trays indoors too, as backup.

KITCHEN

In season

- **Halibut, crab** and **salmon** are now coming in, and **shrimp, whitebait** and **lobster** are in season.
- The first **peas** from the garden start to come through, as well as early **radishes** and the very first spears of **asparagus**. **Rocket, spring onions, watercress** and **wild nettles** can be found, and the last of the **purple sprouting broccoli**.
- There is still plenty of **rhubarb** to be had.
- **Spring lamb** is available, with the first meat coming from the south-west of the country. It is very tender and succulent, and mild in flavour.

Ingredient of the month – Jersey Royals

The extreme south-facing slopes of Jersey have been cropping the earliest, most tender potatoes of the season for around 130 years. The soil is light and well drained on the steepest fields, known as *côtils*, which slope down to the beaches, so it warms quickly in the spring sun. There is little risk of frost because of proximity to the sea so the potatoes are planted early, grow fast, soft and sweet, and are dug early; these best fields' crops have to be lifted by hand, as machinery cannot cope with the gradient. If you spot some, buy them and boil them up with a sprig of mint the same day, and eat them with a little butter and salt, or with sorrel.

Eggs and Easter

The association of eggs with Easter is directly related to the Lent fast. Lent was once a month-long foray into veganism for everyone in the land, with all meat and animal products out of bounds. Of all the raw animal products, eggs keep best, and it would have been fairly easy to build up a surplus ready for the breaking of the fast on Easter Sunday morning. There might even be so many that some could be given to children to decorate.

But eggs and this moment in the year go back even further. This is a time of burgeoning fertility and promise in the landscape, and a particularly important and joyous moment in the year to our farming ancestors, after the trials of winter. Not only are eggs particularly abundant at this time of year, they also encapsulate this moment of renewal and birth rather perfectly. It is thought that the pagan feast of Ëostre once marked this moment, in celebration of all of the new life and foods that tell us that the farming year has begun, and it may even have provided a handy pre-existing celebration of reawakening and hope with which to merge the story of Jesus's resurrection.

RECIPES

Eggs Benedict

We are used to having eggs all year round, but like any bird, chickens want to lay in spring, and eggs are particularly rich and nutritious now, and mightily plentiful. Put a perfectly poached new season's egg on a pedestal of early spinach, smoked ham and toasted muffin, and crown it with a silky (egg-based) hollandaise sauce – a luxurious way to use up a surplus.

Serves 2

Ingredients

200 g baby spinach

Knob of butter

Whole nutmeg, for grating

Salt and pepper

2 English muffins

4 very fresh eggs

75 g smoked ham

For the hollandaise sauce

100 g butter

2 egg yolks

1 tbsp lemon juice

1 tsp Dijon mustard

White wine vinegar

Method

Wash the spinach well, drop it into a large saucepan over
a medium heat and close the lid. The leaves will quickly
collapse and cook in their own steam. Remove from the
heat, tip into a colander and use the back of a large spoon
to squeeze out excess liquid. Chop the spinach roughly, then
return to the pan with the knob of butter, a fresh grating
of nutmeg, and salt and pepper to taste. Keep warm. Next
make the hollandaise sauce. Melt the butter in a pan. Place
a heatproof bowl over a pan of simmering water and whisk
together the yolks, lemon juice and mustard, then slowly add
the butter, whisking to emulsify as you go. If it gets too thick
you can add a little water. Add a dash of vinegar, and salt and
pepper to season. Keep warm over the simmering water.
Split and toast the muffins. Bring a large pan of water to the
boil and add a splash of vinegar. Turn the heat down to its
lowest, then crack each egg into a cup and lower it gently into
the water. Cook for 3 minutes exactly, then lift and drain onto
kitchen paper. Put a bed of spinach and ham onto each half of
muffin, and top each with an egg and the hollandaise sauce.

Wild greens pesto

Dollop this on egg dishes or alongside sausages or baked chicken. If you are using nettle tops, be sure to first blanch them in boiling water for a minute to remove the sting.

Makes 1 jar full
Ingredients
1 large handful of wild garlic leaves or other wild greens, washed well, nettles blanched, drained and patted dry
60 g blanched and toasted hazelnuts
60 g hard goat's cheese, finely grated
150 ml extra virgin olive oil
Juice of ¼ lemon
Salt and pepper

Method
Put the leaves, nuts and cheese into a food processor and blitz just enough to leave a little texture. Add the olive oil and lemon juice, and salt and pepper to taste. Blitz to combine. Serve immediately or spoon into a jar and cover with a layer of oil before storing in the fridge for a few days.

Wild greens

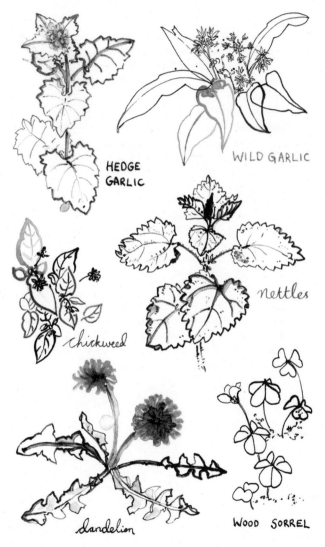

HEDGE GARLIC

WILD GARLIC

chickweed

nettles

dandelion

WOOD SORREL

A

NATURE

Look out for:

- The arrival of the first swallows and swifts later in the month. Listen out for swifts' distinctive, high-pitched, piercing call as they wheel around the sky.
- This is a moment of great movement for many other birds. House martins, whitethroats, willow warblers, nightingales and cuckoos also return from their winter journeys, while visiting geese, swans and waders leave for cooler climates.
- Although not yet at full volume, the dawn chorus is increasing all the time. This month blackbirds and song thrushes join the party.
- On woodland floors look out for the flowers of wood anemones and, late in the month, the first bluebells.
- Cowslips, hairy violet and pasque flower are in flower on chalk downland, and spectacular shows of snake's-head fritillaries can be seen on damp meadows.
- Peacock, speckled wood and orange-tip butterflies emerge.

Wild garlic

This is the short, sweet spell on the woodland floor when warmth has increased enough for growth, but the canopy has not yet expanded enough to shade out the understorey. Plants leap into life to take advantage of this temporal niche, leafing up, blooming, setting seed and vanishing by high summer. Wild garlic is one of those plants that in some parts of the country emerged last month, but is most certainly in leaf everywhere now and will be in flower by the end of the month and into May. It is a native plant and considered an indicator of ancient woodland, especially when it grows, as it often does, alongside bluebells. This is the time to visit the woods to pick and use wild garlic: it is at its best when it is young and fresh and can be past its finest by the time the flowers appear. It is not hard to find, carpeting huge swathes of woodland and smelling strongly of garlic, and you should cut – not pull – yourself a good few handfuls to use chopped in scrambled eggs, in savoury scones, or stir fries. Wild-garlic gathering is a great place to start if you are new to foraging, as it is easy to find and to use, but do take care not to confuse the leaves with lily of the valley or autumn crocus. The smell is the best indicator.

May

● **1** May Day

● **1** Beltane (pagan celebration)

● **7** Early May bank holiday

● **7** 7th–9th: Rogationtide/beating the bounds

● **9** Liberation Day (local holiday, Guernsey and Jersey)

● **10** Ascension Day

● **16** First day of Ramadan (Muslim month of prayer and fasting)

● **20** Shavuot (Jewish Festival of Weeks)

● **20** Whitsun

● **22** 22nd–26th: Chelsea Flower Show

● **28** Spring bank holiday

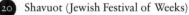

May is a month when our pagan roots poke above the surface a little more determinedly than usual. May Day, once called Beltane, is a festival we can't seem to resist celebrating, and there still exist rich traditions involving flower-crowned girls, green and beribboned men, hobby horses and more, up and down the country. Perhaps it is down to the irresistible nature of this moment in the year: early May is when the slow and halting progress from winter to summer finally becomes a stampede, and fresh green leaves and white blossom break out all over. Why wouldn't we celebrate?

The month is possibly named after the Greek goddess Maia, associated with fertility, the land, and growth. More prosaically the Anglo-Saxons called it Thrimilci, the month when cows were eating the abundant new grass and could be milked three times a day. Hawthorn, known as mayflower, is the dominant and abundant flower of the month, filling the countryside with a white froth, and a sure sign that finally, from time to time, clouts can be cast.

THE SKY

Moon phases

3rd quarter – 2nd May	
New moon – 8th May	
1st quarter – 17th May	
Full moon – 24th May	

M

In the night sky this month

6th & 7th	Eta Aquarids meteor shower produces about 40 meteors an hour at its peak, radiating from the constellation Aquarius. The waning moon will block the fainter tracks.
9th	Jupiter is at opposition, and so is at its largest and brightest tonight, but good for weeks either side of this date. Tonight its highest point (when it is most easily seen) will be 22 degrees above the southern horizon at 1 a.m.
17th	Close approach of moon with Venus tonight, 18 degrees above the western horizon from 10 p.m.
27th	Close approach of moon with Jupiter tonight, from 10.30 p.m., 17 degrees above the south-eastern horizon.

Constellation of the month – Leo

This is a good month in which to view Leo: look to the
south at around 11 p.m. and you may pick out the distinctive
asterism the Sickle, which makes up the lion's head.
Alternatively you can find Leo by following the 'pointer stars'
in the Big Dipper (see March constellation) in the opposite
direction to the North Star. Denebola, the lion's tail star and
the second brightest star in the constellation, was known
by Persian astronomers as the 'weather changer': when it
becomes visible in autumn the weather will cool, and when
it leaves the night sky in late spring, warm weather is on its
way. Regulus is the brightest star in Leo, and if you look at
it through binoculars on a clear night you can see that it is
actually a double star.

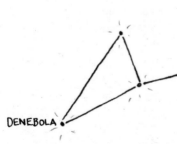

REGULUS

DENEBOLA

Moon rise and set

	London		Glasgow		
	Rise	Set	Rise	Set	
1st	21.55	06.44	22.29	06.47	
2nd	22.59	07.14	23.36	07.14	
3rd	23.57	07.50	–	07.46	
4th	–	08.31	00.36	08.26	
5th	00.49	09.19	01.28	09.14	
6th	01.33	10.13	02.12	10.09	
7th	02.11	11.11	02.48	11.10	
8th	02.44	12.14	03.17	12.16	3rd quarter
9th	03.12	13.19	03.41	13.25	
10th	03.37	14.27	04.02	14.37	
11th	04.00	15.36	04.21	15.51	
12th	04.22	16.49	04.39	17.07	
13th	04.45	18.03	04.58	18.27	
14th	05.10	19.21	05.19	19.49	
15th	05.39	20.39	05.44	21.12	new moon
16th	06.14	21.57	06.14	22.34	
17th	06.56	23.09	06.53	23.48	
18th	07.49	–	07.44	–	
19th	08.52	00.12	08.47	00.52	
20th	10.03	01.04	10.00	01.41	
21st	11.18	01.46	11.19	02.20	
22nd	12.34	02.20	12.40	02.49	1st quarter
23rd	13.49	02.48	14.00	03.13	
24th	15.03	03.13	15.18	03.33	
25th	16.15	03.36	16.35	03.52	
26th	17.26	03.58	17.50	04.10	
27th	18.35	04.21	19.04	04.29	
28th	19.43	04.46	20.16	04.05	
29th	20.48	05.15	21.24	05.15	full moon
30th	21.49	05.48	22.27	05.45	
31st	22.43	06.26	23.23	06.21	

M

WEATHER

May's weather is fickle and changeable: a glorious premonition of true summer for a spell, followed quickly by a chilly blanket of cloud. This is because the prevailing westerly airflow over north-west Europe is at its weakest in May, leaving cold airstreams from the east to move in. Temperatures rise this month and growth is irresistible, as evidenced by the explosion of green in the countryside, but this is also the month of the cold snap and the late frost, and although these are relatively rare in the south, gardeners in the north in particular are not safely out of the woods until the end of the month. Dramatic thunderstorms peak in June, July and August, but May is the next most thunderous month, and hailstorms are not uncommon, as anyone who has attempted to build a leaf-perfect Chelsea Flower Show garden will attest.

Average temperatures (°c):	London 14, Glasgow 11
Average sunshine hours per day:	London 6, Glasgow 6
Average days rainfall:	London 15, Glasgow 19
Average rainfall total (mm):	London 50, Glasgow 60

Day length
During the course of May, day length increases by:

1 hour and 27 minutes, to 16 hours and 17 minutes (London)

1 hour and 46 minutes, to 17 hours and 7 minutes (Glasgow)

Sunrise and set

	London		Glasgow	
	Rise	Set	Rise	Set
1st	05.33	20.24	05.34	20.56
2nd	05.31	20.25	05.32	20.58
3rd	05.29	20.27	05.30	21.00
4th	05.27	20.29	05.27	21.02
5th	05.25	20.30	05.25	21.04
6th	05.24	20.32	05.23	21.06
7th	05.22	20.33	05.21	21.07
8th	05.20	20.35	05.19	21.09
9th	05.18	20.37	05.17	21.11
10th	05.17	20.38	05.15	21.13
11th	05.15	20.40	05.13	21.15
12th	05.14	20.41	05.11	21.17
13th	05.12	20.43	05.09	21.19
14th	05.10	20.44	05.07	21.21
15th	05.09	20.46	05.05	21.23
16th	05.07	20.47	05.03	21.25
17th	05.06	20.49	05.02	21.26
18th	05.05	20.50	05.00	21.28
19th	05.03	20.52	04.58	21.30
20th	05.02	20.53	04.56	21.32
21st	05.01	20.54	04.55	21.34
22nd	04.59	20.56	04.53	21.35
23rd	04.58	20.57	04.52	21.37
24th	04.57	20.59	04.50	21.39
25th	04.56	21.00	04.49	21.40
26th	04.55	21.01	04.47	21.42
27th	04.54	21.02	04.46	21.43
28th	04.53	21.04	04.45	21.45
29th	04.52	21.05	04.44	21.46
30th	04.51	21.06	04.42	21.48
31st	04.50	21.07	04.41	21.49

M

THE SEA

Average sea temperature

Orkney:	9.2°C
Scarborough:	9.8°C
Blackpool:	11°C
Brighton:	11.4°C
Penzance:	12°C

Spring and neap tides

The spring tide is the most extreme tide of the month, with the highest rises and falls, and the neap tide is the least extreme, with the smallest. Exact timings vary around the coast, but expect each around the following dates:

Spring tides:	1st–2nd, 16th–17th and 30th–31st
Neap tides:	9th–10th and 23rd–24th

Wild swimming season commences

If you are hard as nails you may have been swimming in the sea and rivers all winter and early spring, but for most of us this is the time when we start to be tempted in by warmer weather. The sea around our coasts never reaches anything approaching warm, struggling to get above 17°C even in September, its warmest month, and so a swim at any time of year will be a bracing cold-water experience. But there is a gradual temperature increase from now on that makes a summer swim less challenging than a winter one. Cold is shocking to the body and despite everyone believing that diving in and getting it over with is the best way, it is not the safest, especially for delicate hearts. Let your body get used to the cold, taking a full two minutes to submerge completely. After only two or three sea or river dips you will find yourself remarkably acclimatised and mildly addicted.

THE GARDEN

Planting by the moon

As the moon goes through its phases, it moves the water on earth to create the tides, and many believe, not unreasonably, that it has other hidden but equally consequential effects on the natural world. If it can move the oceans perhaps it can move ground water too, and even the small amounts of water trapped in each plant. Planting by the moon is a method of gardening that taps into and utilises the rising and falling of water with the moon's phases. When the moon is new and not visible in the sky, the strength of its gravitational pull on the earth is at its weakest. This is considered a good time to sow plants that develop below ground (root crops) and that are slow to germinate, because soil moisture is steadily increasing. Faster-germinating plants that crop above ground should be sown in the run up to full moon, as this is when the pull is at its strongest and so groundwater will be at its highest. The full moon is also the best time to harvest crops for immediate use, as they are at their juiciest. After full moon the moon's pull starts to wane and groundwater drops, and these are good times for pruning (to minimise sap loss), and harvesting for storage (skins are drier and tougher). If you would like to give the system a try, you will find the relevant dates and jobs in the garden section of each month of this almanac.

3rd quarter to new moon: 8th–15th. Prune. Harvest for storage. Fertilise and mulch the soil.

New moon to 1st quarter: 15th–22nd. Sow crops that develop below ground. Dig the soil.

1st quarter to full moon: 22nd–29th. Sow crops that develop above ground. Plant seedlings and young plants.

Full moon to 3rd quarter: 29th–31st. Harvest crops for immediate eating. Harvest fruit.

Jobs in the garden

- Move pots of tulips into prime positions by your front door and flanking garden steps. Apply a liquid feed to any bulbs that have finished flowering, and remove spent flower heads, to encourage more flowers next year.
- Track down small plants of cut flower chrysanthemums from specialist growers and plant them out for late summer and autumn bunches.
- Thin out direct-sown seedlings in the vegetable patch, lifting and discarding seedlings that have been sown too thick, to give crops space to fill out. Do this in a couple of stages, some taken now, some in a couple of weeks, in case of slug attacks or other calamities.

Glut of the month – asparagus

Asparagus is up! Enjoy this brief and delicious crop while it lasts.

- You will want to eat most of your asparagus simply steamed or very lightly boiled for just a few minutes. They love butter and eggs. Toss in butter, or dip into soft-boiled eggs like soldiers, or top with a hollandaise sauce.
- Asparagus takes particularly well to roasting, useful for when the split-second timing of steaming would be tricky. Toss in olive oil and salt and roast for 20 minutes, then pile on top of a bed of braised lentils and buffalo mozzarella.
- Try it raw, shaved into fine slivers, in a salad with new peas, mangetout, radish and Little Gem lettuce, topped with shavings of Parmesan.

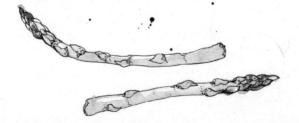

Preparing baby artichokes

When artichokes are tiny and tender, as they are this month, much of the fuss of preparing them is avoided, as they have not yet developed the 'choke' that needs to be removed when they grow larger. To prepare your baby artichokes you will need a bowl of water with the juice of half a lemon squeezed into it, a serrated knife and a sharp paring knife.

Scrub the outside of the artichokes first under running water. Shorten the stem to about 2½ cm and use the serrated knife to slice off the top third of stiff, spiky, dark green 'petals'. Peel away a couple of layers of hard green outer 'petals' until the soft and paler green and yellow ones beneath are revealed, and then pare away any rough leftover pieces and the skin from the stem. Slice the artichoke in half lengthways and drop into the lemon water to prevent browning. When you have prepared a few, drop them into boiling water and boil for around 10 minutes or until you can easily pierce the base of the artichoke with a toothpick or knife. Incorporate them into a pasta dish or eat them in a salad with best olive oil and wedges of lemon and salt.

Garden task – deal with slugs

May is the month for planting out seedlings. It is also when slugs are at their most voracious, and can wipe out a whole row of painstakingly nurtured new seedlings in a single night. There is almost no point in growing anything from seed if you are not going to take on the slug menace, so be ready.

There are a number of options available, none of which will work perfectly, so carry out as many as you can: belt and braces. Slug pellets are effective but problematic. Old-fashioned ones based on metaldehyde have been proven dangerous to wildlife, and questions are now being raised around new, supposedly organic, iron phosphate-based pellets, so avoid if possible. Go for good soil first. If plants struggle in hard, poor soil, they will be vulnerable for longer. Dig in compost or well-rotted manure and young plants will romp out of harm's way.

Slug traps are gruesome but help to reduce numbers. Cut a hole a few centimetres up one side of a plastic milk bottle. 'Plant' it shallowly in the ground (leaving a lip so that beetles and other innocents do not wander in) and fill the base with beer. Slugs are attracted to the beer and climb in and drown. Night-time torchlit veg patch raids can be very effective, when slugs are at their most active. Collect them in a bucket and dispose of them as you will. Use plastic collars with lips around larger plants such as courgettes, and sprinkle bran around smaller seedlings. It all sounds like hard work, but this phase will not last forever. Once your seedlings have grown into young plants they become less attractive to slugs and can shrug off a bit of damage. A little vigilance and action now will pay off.

Garden slugs

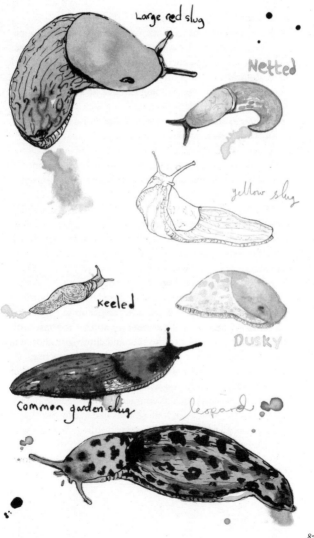

Large red slug

Netted

yellow slug

keeled

Dusky

common garden slug

leopard

M

KITCHEN

In season

- In the vegetable patch some of the treats of the year are now at their height: **asparagus, sorrel, peas, broad beans, radish, chives** and **chive flowers**, and **young spinach**. Although it is tempting to leave tiny **globe artichoke** heads to grow bigger, they are at their best when small (and they will quickly produce more).
- Although you may not have produced your own **new potatoes** yet, they are at the height of their season in the greengrocers.
- **Rhubarb** is still good and **British strawberries** start to reach the greengrocers. **Apricots** arrive from France.
- **Crab, sardines, plaice** and **mackerel** are all in season.

Ingredient of the month – green garlic

If you planted your garlic cloves last autumn, you will be harvesting your main crop of garlic for storage in the summer, but you can take a few of the young 'green' bulbs now for their fresh, mild flavour. Gardener's perks.

Pull a bulb up and you will see that your green garlic has not yet split into cloves. It has not even started to form the papery outer skin that makes it ready for storage and so it will not keep. You won't want to dig too many as it will reduce your final crop, but take a few and try them roasted until caramelised, shaved raw over salads, or gently sautéed and whizzed into a soup with peas.

FESTIVITIES

The May Queen

The countryside in early May is an explosion of green and froth, all fresh, young, burgeoning life. The May Queen is the personification of this moment. She is traditionally young and beautiful, not a child and not quite a woman, but on the cusp. There is an innocence and purity about her crowning but she is not guileless, and just as the perfect white blossom that she wears on her crown will soon be pollinated, so the May Queen is on the verge of her own awakening. This is captured in Tennyson's melodramatic poem 'The May Queen', where our soon-to-be queen at first talks of garlands and white dresses but is soon flirting cruelly, and then pairing up with one of the 'bolder lads' she meets on the day. Such flagrant enjoyment of her own beauty and youth cannot go unpunished, and in true Victorian style we fast-forward to our saucy heroine dying of an unnamed illness mysteriously related to her 'wild and wayward' ways. That'll teach her for messing with those shepherd boys.

A less cruel but still problematic fate meets the Queen of the May in the traditional folk song of the same name. Out gathering May blossom, she meets a man who convinces her to sit with him on the mossy green bank – the gentlest possible euphemism. But it's all OK because the next day he marries her so that 'the world should have nothing to say'. Lucky girl. The May Queen starts the day as sweet and innocent as the blossom in her crown and ends it, well... a little more fruitful.

The May Queen persists in May Day fairs up and down the country. This is a moment for fun, frolics and petal-strewn mossy green banks. The birds and the bees, the flowers and the trees are all at it. But as the stories make clear, things must soon turn serious, and the real work of the year – the swelling, maturing and reproducing – must begin.

RECIPES

Rhubarb, strawberry and apricot pastry

These three fruits are perfect at the moment; their colours glow when they are roasted together and spread across a bed of honeyed mascarpone.

Ingredients

1 sheet puff pastry
1 egg yolk, beaten
2 stems rhubarb
8 apricots
4 tbsp orange juice
200 g strawberries, hulled
250 g mascarpone cheese
1 tbsp honey

Method

Preheat your oven to 200°C/400°F/gas mark 6. Lay out the pastry sheet on a piece of baking parchment on a baking sheet and brush the edges with water. Fold a narrow margin all the way around to form a rim, and paint it with the egg yolk. Prick the base of the tart all over with a fork. Bake for 15 minutes or until the edges are risen up and brown and the centre sandy-coloured and cooked through. Remove from the oven and leave to cool. Chop the rhubarb into 5-cm pieces, halve the apricots and remove their stones, and put all, along with the strawberries and the orange juice, into a bowl. Turn the fruit so all is moistened by the orange juice and tip into a baking tray. Bake for 15–20 minutes, until the apricots and the rhubarb are tender and the juice of the strawberries is running. Remove from the oven and leave to cool. Mix the mascarpone and the honey and spread it over the cooled base, then arrange the cooled fruit on top, before pouring over any strawberry-coloured juices.

NATURE

Look out for:
- Spectacular sprays of hawthorn blossom in every hedgerow, turning the countryside soft and white. Elder and cow parsley add to the froth.
- Bluebells are in full swing, creating hazy blue carpets across woodland floors.
- Sea cliffs are noisy and busy with seabirds breeding and feeding their young.
- All of the trees are in leaf now, with young, fresh, green growth. Ash is the last to break bud.
- Dandelions flower fat and golden in every crack in every pavement. Daisies are sprinkled liberally across lawns.
- Meadows are colourful and filled with flowers: yellow rattle, buttercup, meadow vetchling, ivy-leaved toadflax, and spotted orchids.
- Verges are full of flower: alongside the cow parsley look for red campion, white dead-nettles and greater stitchwort.
- Watch for Adonis, chalkhill and common blue butterflies.
- Damselflies and dragonflies emerge mid-month from vegetation at the edges of ponds and rivers.

The dawn chorus
The dawn chorus reaches its noisy and joyful peak in May as birds sing their hearts out for mates and territory. At dawn the air is at its stillest, and sound carries well. Birds want to mate and raise their chicks during the warmest months of the year so each morning the male birds frantically try to outdo each other. Kicking off as early as 3 a.m., the birds join in in a predictable order. If you find yourself lying awake listening, see if you can identify as follows: blackbirds (mellow, flutelike, but often with a harsh note at the end), robins (a melodious 'twiddle-ooh, twiddle-eedee'), wrens (a loud warble around five seconds long, ending in a trill), song thrushes (musical and penetrating, with lots of repetition and some grating and chattering sounds), chaffinches (short, fast, rattling song, ending in a flourish) and tree sparrows (incessant cheeps and chirps).

June

- **1** Start of meteorological summer

- **10** Laylatal-Qadr (Muslim 'Night of Power')

- **15** Eid al-Fitr (feast day at the end of Ramadan, the Muslim month of prayer and fasting)

- **17** Father's Day

- **21** Summer solstice/Midsummer's Day/Litha

- **21** Start of astronomical summer

- **27** 27th June to 10th July – Wimbledon

June is true summer: strawberries, roses and rainy picnics, ice cream and sunburnt shoulders. Meteorological summer begins on the 1st, astronomical summer on the 21st, the countryside is full and fresh, and gardens and hedgerows are bursting with colour: if you want your garden to look wonderful in June then you can hardly fail, for everything flowers in June. June of course contains the most daylight of any month, and the longest day and shortest night. But there's the rub: here we are, just getting into the swing of things, and suddenly the pinnacle is reached. After Midsummer's Day on the 21st we start the slow slide towards autumn, and June's midsummer celebrations are tinged with that knowledge. Happily, however, the thermal lag in the seas and land means that our warmest months are ahead of us. We can cast aside niggling thoughts of the dark half of the year, at least for now, and revel in the warmth and light of the moment.

The month may have been named after the Roman goddess of marriage, Juno, and it is certainly a month that lends itself to optimistic outdoor gatherings and celebrations. The Anglo-Saxons called it *sera monath* (dry month). Perhaps things were different then, or perhaps the Anglo-Saxons were as hopeful and foolish about June as we are.

THE SKY

Moon phases

3rd quarter – 2nd June

New moon – 8th June

1st quarter – 17th June

Full moon – 24th June

In the night sky this month

1st	Close approach of moon with Saturn tonight, at their highest at 3 a.m., 16 degrees above the southern horizon.
16th	Close approach of thin crescent moon with Venus tonight, 22 degrees above the western horizon from 10 p.m.
23rd	Close approach of moon with Jupiter tonight, from 10.30 p.m., 17 degrees above the south-eastern horizon.
27th	Saturn is at opposition, and so is at its largest and brightest tonight, but good for weeks either side of this date. Tonight its highest point (when it is most easily seen) is at 1.15 a.m., 16 degrees above the southern horizon.

Constellation of the month – Cassiopeia

As we move through the longest day and the shortest night there is so much light in the sky that constellations become harder to pick out, but the increasing light is matched by an increasing warmth that makes night lingering more enjoyable. Cassiopeia is bright enough to still stand out, and resides in the darker part of the sky at prime star-watching time. Look to the north-east at around 11 p.m. and halfway between the Pole Star and the horizon you will see Cassiopeia's distinctive zigzag of bright stars. Cassiopeia was a vain and boastful queen in Greek mythology, punished by Poseidon for her wicked ways and forced to wheel forever more around the Pole Star.

Moon rise and set

	London		Glasgow		
	Rise	Set	Rise	Set	
1st	23.31	07.12	–	07.06	
2nd	–	08.03	00.10	07.58	
3rd	00.12	09.00	00.49	08.57	
4th	00.46	10.01	01.21	10.01	
5th	01.15	11.04	01.46	11.08	
6th	01.41	12.10	02.08	12.18	3rd quarter
7th	02.04	13.17	02.27	13.30	
8th	02.25	14.27	02.45	14.44	
9th	02.47	15.39	03.03	16.00	
10th	03.11	16.54	03.22	17.20	
11th	03.37	18.12	03.44	18.42	
12th	04.08	19.31	04.10	20.06	
13th	04.46	20.47	04.44	21.26	new moon
14th	05.34	21.57	05.30	22.37	
15th	06.34	22.56	06.28	23.35	
16th	07.44	23.44	07.40	–	
17th	09.00	–	09.00	00.20	
18th	10.19	00.22	10.23	00.53	
19th	11.37	00.53	11.46	01.20	
20th	12.52	01.19	13.06	01.41	1st quarter
21st	14.05	01.42	14.24	02.00	
22nd	15.17	02.05	15.39	02.19	
23rd	16.26	02.27	16.53	02.37	
24th	17.34	02.51	18.05	02.57	
25th	18.39	03.18	19.14	03.20	
26th	19.41	03.49	20.19	03.47	
27th	20.38	04.25	21.18	04.21	
28th	21.28	05.08	22.08	05.02	full moon
29th	22.11	05.57	22.50	05.51	
30th	22.48	06.52	23.24	06.48	

J

The phases of dusk

There are many beautifully poetic names for dusk and
twilight – evenglome, dimmet, the gloaming, simmer dim in
Scotland, the dimpsy in Devon – and for Muslims dusk takes
on a particular weight this month, as it is the moment each
day when they can break their Ramadan fast.

Dusk is also more complicated than you might think, and it
has three stages. Civil twilight is the time between sunset and
the moment that the sun reaches 6 degrees below the horizon.
When 6 degrees is reached (civil dusk), civil authorities
traditionally switched on street lighting. Nautical twilight
is the spell when the sun is between 6 and 12 degrees below
the horizon, and is the time when both the horizon and the
principal navigational stars can be seen, so allowing the use of
a sextant for navigation. Astronomical twilight is the period
when the sun is between 12 and 18 degrees below the horizon:
there is still a little light in the sky, and many of the brighter
stars can be seen. From 23rd May until 21st July in London,
astronomical twilight lasts all night. The same is true for
Glasgow from 5th May until 8th August, except for the
spell between 2nd June and 10th July, when the even lighter
nautical twilight lasts all night.

WEATHER

We hope for 'flaming June' but 'June monsoon' is sadly a
far more likely occurrence. In June, changes in temperatures
in land masses and in atmospheric circulation around the
world often create a strong pattern of westerlies which
drive wet weather across the UK. The month will often
start fine and warm and then deteriorate into rainy weather
around mid-June, causing misery as it runs straight into the
season of summer festivals, fetes and sports fixtures. This
feels particularly cruel when June marks both the start of
meteorological summer (1st June) and the summer solstice
(21st June). Occasionally a heat wave will buck the trend, but
nearly three out of four Junes are wet, so hope to need sun
hats but take brollies too. Temperatures at least are rising fast.

Average temperatures (°C):	London 16, Glasgow 13
Average sunshine hours per day:	London 7, Glasgow 5
Average days rainfall:	London 13, Glasgow 20
Average rainfall total (mm):	London 53, Glasgow 70

Day length

During the course of May, day length increases by:

19 minutes up to its longest at 16 hours and 38 minutes on the
21st, and then shortens by 4 minutes by the end of the month
(London).

25 minutes up to its longest at 17 hours 35 minutes on the
21st, and then shortens by 6 minutes by the end of the month
(Glasgow).

Sunrise and set

	London		Glasgow	
	Rise	Set	Rise	Set
1st	04.49	21.08	04.40	21.50
2nd	04.48	21.09	04.39	21.52
3rd	04.48	21.10	04.38	21.53
4th	04.47	21.11	04.37	21.54
5th	04.46	21.12	04.36	21.55
6th	04.46	21.13	04.36	21.56
7th	04.45	21.14	04.35	21.58
8th	04.45	21.15	04.34	21.59
9th	04.44	21.16	04.34	22.00
10th	04.44	21.16	04.33	22.00
11th	04.44	21.17	04.32	22.01
12th	04.43	21.18	04.32	22.02
13th	04.43	21.18	04.32	22.03
14th	04.43	21.19	04.31	22.03
15th	04.43	21.19	04.31	22.04
16th	04.43	21.20	04.31	22.05
17th	04.43	21.20	04.31	22.05
18th	04.43	21.21	04.31	22.05
19th	04.43	21.21	04.31	22.06
20th	04.43	21.21	04.31	22.06
21st	04.43	21.22	04.31	22.06
22nd	04.43	21.22	04.31	22.07
23rd	04.44	21.22	04.32	22.07
24th	04.44	21.22	04.32	22.07
25th	04.44	21.22	04.33	22.07
26th	04.45	21.22	04.33	22.07
27th	04.45	21.22	04.34	22.06
28th	04.46	21.22	04.34	22.06
29th	04.46	21.21	04.35	22.06
30th	04.47	21.21	04.36	22.05

THE SEA

Average sea temperature

Orkney:	11.1°C
Scarborough:	12.7°C
Blackpool:	13.5°C
Brighton:	13.6°C
Penzance:	14.2°C

Spring and neap tides

The spring tide is the most extreme tide of the month, with the highest rises and falls, and the neap tide is the least extreme, with the smallest. Exact timings vary around the coast, but expect each around the following dates:

Spring tides:	14th–15th and 29th–30th
Neap tides:	7th–8th and 21st–22nd

Mackerel migration

Mackerel migrate around the coastline in June and throughout the summer months. There are two roughly distinct groups: the North Sea stock overwinter in deep water along the edge of the continental shelf to the north and east of Shetland, migrate south to spawn, and spend the summer in the central North Sea close to the east coast, before returning to their overwintering areas in late summer; the western stock overwinter off of the Irish continental shelf, and migrate to spawn and summer in the Celtic Sea and along the west coast. Mackerel are plentiful, easy to catch and delicious.

THE GARDEN

Planting by the moon

Full moon to 3rd quarter: 1st–6th. Harvest crops for immediate eating. Harvest fruit.

3rd quarter to new moon: 6th–13th. Prune. Harvest for storage. Fertilise and mulch the soil.

New moon to 1st quarter: 13th–20th. Sow crops that develop below ground. Dig the soil.

1st quarter to full moon: 20th–28th. Sow crops that develop above ground. Plant seedlings and young plants.

Full moon to 3rd quarter: 28th–30th. Harvest crops for immediate eating. Harvest fruit.

Jobs in the garden

- Sweet peas are flowering now and you must pick them frequently in order to keep them flowering. Plants will quickly switch into seed-producing mode if left unpicked, so make sure you always have a jar of sweet peas on your table. Such a trial.
- Plant plumbago, asters, Japanese anemones, heleniums, rudbeckias and helianthus now for autumn flowers to keep your garden's bees and butterflies happier for longer.
- On the vegetable patch direct-sow: carrots, beetroot, peas, mangetout, kale, Florence fennel, French beans, swede and turnip. Plant out: winter squashes and pumpkins, tomatoes, aubergines, courgettes, sweet potatoes, peppers and chillies.

Glut of the month – gooseberry

Lip-smackingly sour gooseberries are swelling now. Thin them out early in the month, using the small, sharp, pectin-filled early ones for jam and allowing the rest to ripen, soften and sweeten.

- Pork and mackerel have their fattiness and oiliness offset by the sharpness of a gooseberry sauce. Simmer a pan full of berries with a few tablespoons of sugar and a few of water.
- Elderflower adds hints of floral and lemony flavours that rub along very happily indeed with gooseberry. Simmer gooseberries, a little sugar and a head of elderflower together to make the filling for a summery crumble or pie.
- Roasting gooseberries in a little honey sweetens and softens them while caramelising them slightly and allowing them to hold their shape. Tip a spoonful or two of them, still warm, onto thick Greek yoghurt.

Garden task – plant scented pelargoniums

Rub the leaf of one and bring a waft of lemon up to your nose, try another and it is spice and cinnamon, yet another and... cola? Each cut with the sharp tang of the geranium cuttings in your granddad's greenhouse. Scented geraniums are more correctly, though less frequently, known as pelargoniums, and they are the cream of the summer bedding plants. Garden centres are overflowing with little plug plants of fuchsia, petunia and lobelia, all of which can be thrown into a pot or a hanging basket now and will explode into growth and colour, vanishing with the first frosts come autumn. Scented geraniums are similar in temperament and in use, but they are the understated cousins with hidden depths. They make classy temporary basket and pot-fillers, flower delicately and prettily all summer, will waft deliciously as you brush past, and can even be used as a flavouring, the leaves infused in summery drinks, jams and milky puddings (and even in gooseberry crumbles).

'Queen of Lemon' (surely named by an excited five-year-old following their first sniff) is one of the best citrusy varieties, but there are others, among them 'Pink Capitatum' – lime-scented – and 'Orange Fizz'. 'Lady Plymouth' is one of the best looking and most delicious, with grey-green and gold variegated leaves, pale lilac flowers, and a rose-mint fragrance. The leaves of 'Rose of Attar' emit a subtly different old-world rose fragrance when faintly crushed, those of 'Ardwick Cinnamon' are spicy, 'Birdbush Nutty' smells of roasted almonds, 'Candy Dancer' of Turkish delight and so on. There is a whole world of bizarrely and beautifully fragranced pelargoniums, and this is the time to explore it.

Rose flower types

SEMI-DOUBLE
blanc double de Coubert

SINGLE
rosa canina

CUPPED
Alnwick Castle

QUARTERED
tradescant

HYBRID TEA
king's Macc

J

KITCHEN

In season

- You can start picking **broad beans, globe artichokes, French beans, peas, lettuce, Florence fennel** and **carrots**, and you may dig some **new potatoes. Watercress, spring onions** and **radishes** are all ready.
- Summer herbs – **basil, mint, chives** and **dill** – are fresh and perfect now.
- **Strawberries, raspberries, cherries, apricots** and **gooseberries** are at their best this month. **Blackcurrants, white currants** and **redcurrants** are fruiting.
- **Crab, mackerel** and **sardines** are plentiful.
- Fresh, unmatured cheeses such as **ewe's curd, chevre, ricotta** and **feta** are at their finest now, as herds are eating abundant young grass and herbs.

Ingredient of the month – brown crab

Although there are 65 species of British crab, the one you are most likely to find yourself eating is the brown crab, *Cancer pagurus*, with its reddish-brown carapace, pie-crust-shaped top, and black-tipped pincers. Summer is the season, as in winter they are breeding and moulting (the shells do not grow so they have to cast them aside, during which time they are not good eating). They can be found all around the British Isles but Norfolk is particularly famous for them – Cromer crabs are particularly sweet, with a higher proportion of white to brown meat than those caught elsewhere, perhaps due to the presence of a chalk shelf just off of the coast. But crab is pretty wonderful all around the coast. Buy them from the fishmonger as 'dressed' crab, with the meat picked out for you, and use the white meat in salads and pasta dishes and the brown meat spread onto hot buttered toast.

FESTIVITIES

The midsummer fire

June contains a great turning point in the year, as the sun reaches its highest point, pauses there for a moment, and then begins the descent back towards winter. Midsummer was a vastly significant date to our farming ancestors – although it was traditionally celebrated on the 23rd or the 24th of June, rather than on the actual longest day on the 21st – and it was a date regarded with a healthy dose of anxiety, perhaps necessary to spur on preparations for the darker, less bountiful months.

While the idea that our ancestors gathered at Stonehenge and the like to welcome in Midsummer's Day is much disputed, there is far more evidence for the popularity of the midsummer fire. Throughout Britain and Europe bonfires have long been lit as the sun set on Midsummer Eve, in the streets, on high hills, and on farmland. These widespread celebrations generally had three common features: bonfires, torchlit processions, and the rolling of a burning wheel. Bones and rubbish were burned to create smoke to drive away bad spirits, and midsummer fires had a magical quality. Cattle would be driven through them and young men would leap over them for luck. Long-burning kitchen hearth fires would be put out and rekindled using burning brands from the midsummer fire, as if to hold on to the height of summer and to stave away the coming dark for as long as possible. And the burning wheels would be driven down hills by whooping boys, directly representing the sun making its descent, and to fatalistic applause from gathered onlookers: if it is going to happen, let's send it on its way in style.

RECIPES

Elderflower champagne

Don't miss the oh-so-brief chance to create one of the hedgerow delicacies of the year. Pick elderflower heads in the morning, before the bees have stolen all of the sweet nectar, and from trees well away from busy roads. This recipe is quick, easy and a little wild as it makes use of unpredictable natural yeasts.

Ingredients

2 l boiling water
650 g sugar
2 l cold water
Juice and skins of 4 lemons
15 heads of elderflower
2 tbsp white wine vinegar
5 g champagne yeast (if needed)

Method

In a bucket pour the boiling water over the sugar and stir to dissolve. Add the cold water, the lemon skins and juice, and the elderflower heads and cover everything with a muslin. Check it after three days and if it has not started to froth up, add the champagne yeast. Once it has fermented for six days sieve it through a sterilised muslin into a sterilised bucket. Allow the sediment to settle for a few hours and then siphon it into screw-top plastic bottles or swing-top-stopper glass bottles. It is ready to drink after about a week. You can keep it longer – it is beautiful after a couple of months – but it is a good idea to release the pressure once a week to avoid explosions later down the line or to store it in the fridge to slow the build-up.

Atayef stuffed with walnuts A recipe by Nisrin Abuorf

The Muslim holy month of Ramadan runs this year from 16th May to 15th June, beginning and ending at the sighting of the crescent moon. It involves fasting from dawn to sunset, and while areas of Britain with large Muslim populations may be quieter than usual during the day, just before sunset the restaurants start to fill up with hungry customers anticipating the moment they can finally break their fast. At the end of the meal many will have atayef for dessert. This stuffed pancake is well loved but almost never eaten outside of Ramadan, a sort of Muslim equivalent of the mince pie.

Makes 10 pancakes

Ingredients

For the sugar syrup

300 g sugar

150 ml water

1 tsp orange-blossom water

Juice of half a lemon

For the walnut stuffing

150 g roughly crushed walnuts

1 tbsp caster sugar

½ tsp cinnamon

1 tbsp grated coconut

For the pancakes

200 g plain flour

50 g semolina

1 heaped tsp corn flour

1 tbsp caster sugar

| A pinch of salt |
| ½ tsp instant yeast |
| 1 heaped tsp baking powder |
| 150 ml full-fat milk |
| 250 ml warm water |
| 150 g unsalted butter, melted |

Method

Prepare the sugar syrup first. In a pan put the sugar, the water and orange-blossom water and bring to the boil. Once the water starts bubbling pour in the lemon juice, reduce the heat, and simmer for 5 minutes. Remove from the heat.

Blend all of the pancake ingredients except the melted butter together for 3 minutes. If working without a blender, put the dry ingredients into a large bowl, make a well in the centre, and pour in the milk and water in stages, slowly incorporating the dry mix from the edges. The batter is ready when there are lots of bubbles on the surface. In another bowl mix crushed walnuts, sugar, cinnamon and coconut for the stuffing.

Brush a non-stick pan with some of the melted butter and heat until the surface is very hot; then turn the hob down to medium heat. Pour a full ladle into the pan. The pancake should start forming bubbles on the surface. As soon as the surface has dried, take the pancake out and place on a plate. Repeat this process until all the batter is used.

While the pancakes are still warm, stuff each with a teaspoon of stuffing, then close the round pancake disc into a half circle by pinching and pressing the two sides of the pancake. Brush the stuffed pancakes all over with the melted butter then grill until both sides are golden brown and crisp. Pour the cooled syrup over the pancakes and serve immediately.

NATURE

Look out for:
- Hedgerows and verges are full of the first foxglove flowers, wild honeysuckle, dog rose, and blackberry flowers.
- In grassland look out for flowering ox-eye daisies and bird's-foot trefoil.
- Birds will be singing less and spending their energy searching for food for their young chicks.
- June is the best time for visiting the limestone grasslands of the north and the chalk downlands of the south. Look out for bee orchids, common spotted orchids, and pyramidal orchids, as well as cheddar pinks, bellflower, betony, common milkwort, horseshoe vetch and meadow saxifrage.
- This is the height of moth season, and of bat season too, and night walks or moth-watching evenings will be well rewarded.
- Meadow brown and marbled white butterflies can be seen in long grass. And look out for marsh fritillaries.
- Flag irises are in flower around lakes and rivers. Look out for beautiful demoiselles and banded demoiselles taking to the air as they emerge in mid-June.
- Thrift and sheep's-bit are in flower on seaside clifftops.
- Farmland birds that can be seen this month include yellowhammers, corn buntings, linnets, goldfinches and greenfinches.

J

July

8 Sea Sunday (Catholic Church)

12 Battle of the Boyne (local holiday, Northern Ireland)

15 St Swithun's Day

Summer starts to relax in July. The eager young lime-coloured leaves that filled the countryside last month have mellowed to a rich green, and the wheat and barley have started to turn golden, rippled silver by lazy breezes. Butterflies flit and mowers whir, and we start to believe it will always be this way. There are plenty of thunderstorms in July to mess with our idea of what summer should be, but often they will follow spells of warmth – fat droplets on dusty pavements – and bring with them the vibrant fragrance of wet earth after dry heat, an ozone-scented sigh of relief.

July was named to honour Julius Caesar, it being his birth month, and before him it was known as Quintilis, Latin for 'fifth', as this was the fifth month in the Roman year. More expressively, the Anglo-Saxons called it Weodmonath, the month of weeds, or Heymonath, as this is hay-making time.

THE SKY

Moon phases

3rd quarter – 6th July

New moon – 13th July

1st quarter – 19th July

Full moon – 27th July

In the night sky this month

1st	Close approach of the moon and Mars tonight, at its highest at 3.15 a.m., 15 degrees above the southern horizon.
15th	Close approach of the moon with Venus tonight, very thin crescent moon faintly visible around 9.45 p.m. as dusk fades, 11 degrees above the western horizon.
27th	Total lunar eclipse, the moon rises eclipsed between 8.45 p.m. and 9.30 p.m., visible low in east–southeast sky. It will be red in colour, sometimes called a blood moon. Total eclipse ends 10.30 p.m., but there will still be traces of shadow beyond midnight.
27th	Mars is at opposition, and so is at its largest and brightest tonight, but good for weeks either side of this date. Tonight its highest point (when it is most easily seen) will be at 1.30 a.m., 12 degrees above the southern horizon

Asterism of the month – the Summer Triangle

The Summer Triangle is an asterism – an easily recognised group of particularly bright stars – rather than a constellation, and it includes three constellations: Cygnus, Lyra and Aquila. July is its month, when it rides high in the sky all night. As evening falls, look east for sparkling blue-white Vega, the brightest star in the constellation Lyra, the Harp. Left and down you will find Deneb, the brightest star in the constellation Cygnus, the Swan. Right and down from Deneb is Altair, the brightest star in Aquila, the Eagle. Deneb will swing up to become the topmost star as the evening wears on. If you are lucky enough to be stargazing in a dark, rural location you will see the Milky Way ploughing through the centre of the triangle, from Deneb to between Vega and Altair, so once you have familiarised yourself with the Summer Triangle you can use it as a Milky Way pointer, however faintly it can be seen.

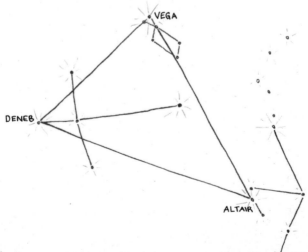

Moon rise and set

	London		Glasgow		
	Rise	Set	Rise	Set	
1st	23.19	07.51	23.51	07.50	
2nd	23.45	08.54	–	08.56	
3rd	–	09.58	00.14	10.05	
4th	00.09	11.04	00.34	11.15	
5th	00.31	12.12	00.52	12.26	
6th	00.52	13.21	01.09	13.40	3rd quarter
7th	01.13	14.32	01.26	14.56	
8th	01.37	15.47	01.46	16.15	
9th	02.05	17.03	02.09	17.36	
10th	02.38	18.20	02.38	18.57	
11th	03.20	19.34	03.17	20.13	
12th	04.14	20.39	04.08	21.19	
13th	05.19	21.34	05.14	22.11	new moon
14th	06.34	22.18	06.32	22.51	
15th	07.55	22.53	07.57	23.21	
16th	09.16	23.22	09.23	23.46	
17th	10.35	23.47	10.47	–	
18th	11.52	–	12.08	00.07	
19th	13.05	00.10	13.26	00.25	1st quarter
20th	14.16	00.33	14.42	00.44	
21st	15.25	00.57	15.55	01.04	
22nd	16.31	01.22	17.05	01.25	
23rd	17.34	01.52	18.11	01.51	
24th	18.33	02.26	19.12	02.22	
25th	19.25	03.06	20.05	03.01	
26th	20.11	03.53	20.50	03.47	
27th	20.49	04.46	21.26	04.41	full moon
28th	21.22	05.44	21.56	05.42	
29th	21.50	06.46	22.20	06.47	
30th	22.14	07.50	22.41	07.55	
31st	22.36	08.55	22.59	09.04	

J

Total lunar eclipse

This month sees a total lunar eclipse visible from when the moon rises on the 27th between 8.45 p.m. and 9.30 p.m. The full eclipse ends at 10.30 p.m. and the last traces of shadow vanish at around 12.30 a.m. on the 28th. A lunar eclipse occurs when the earth is between the moon and the sun, and so casts its shadow across the moon. They are far more common than solar eclipses, when the moon slips between the earth and the sun. However, only one in three lunar eclipses is a full eclipse like this one, rather than just a section of the earth's shadow passing across the moon, and this should make for a dramatic effect. Full lunar eclipses are sometimes called 'blood moons' because the moon takes on shades of red and orange. Also look out for a blue band towards the end of totality.

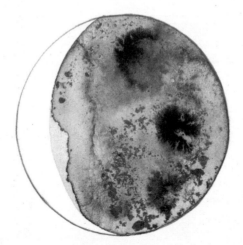

Sunrise and set

	London		*Glasgow*	
	Rise	Set	Rise	Set
1st	04.48	21.21	04.36	22.05
2nd	04.48	21.21	04.37	22.04
3rd	04.49	21.20	04.38	22.04
4th	04.50	21.20	04.39	22.03
5th	04.51	21.19	04.40	22.02
6th	04.51	21.19	04.41	22.02
7th	04.52	21.18	04.42	22.01
8th	04.53	21.17	04.43	22.00
9th	04.54	21.17	04.45	21.59
10th	04.55	21.16	04.46	21.58
11th	04.54	21.15	04.47	21.57
12th	04.57	21.14	04.48	21.56
13th	04.58	21.13	04.50	21.55
14th	05.00	21.12	04.51	21.54
15th	05.01	21.11	04.53	21.52
16th	05.02	21.10	04.54	21.51
17th	05.03	21.09	04.56	21.50
18th	05.04	21.08	04.57	21.48
19th	05.06	21.07	04.59	21.47
20th	05.07	21.06	05.00	21.45
21st	05.08	21.05	05.02	21.44
22nd	05.10	21.03	05.04	21.42
23rd	05.11	21.02	05.05	21.40
24th	05.12	21.01	05.07	21.39
25th	05.14	20.59	05.09	21.37
26th	05.15	20.58	05.11	21.35
27th	05.17	20.56	05.12	21.33
28th	05.18	20.55	05.14	21.32
29th	05.20	20.53	05.16	21.30
30th	05.21	20.52	05.18	21.28
31st	05.23	20.50	05.20	21.26

J

WEATHER

St Swithun's day if thou dost rain
For forty days it will remain
St Swithun's day if thou be fair
For forty days 'twill rain nae mare

Everybody knows that the saying about St Swithun's Day, which falls on 15th July, never comes true. If it rains on the 15th we are very unlikely to then be subject to 40 days of rain, and, likewise, if it is sunny we are not guaranteed a scorcher of a summer. However, there is a grain of truth that may have inspired the legend, in that summer weather patterns established by mid-July often persist well into August. The day itself won't tell you much, but the general trend might. Clearly, July can be beautiful, warm and sunny, and many of Britain's highest temperatures have occurred in July, but the probability of rain does increase as the month goes on. July is one of the stormiest months, with thunderstorms sparked by high temperatures.

Average temperatures (°C):	London 19, Glasgow 15
Average sunshine hours per day:	London 6, Glasgow 5
Average days rainfall:	London 14, Glasgow 21
Average rainfall total (mm):	London 41, Glasgow 70

Day length

During the course of July, day length decreases by:

1 hour and 6 minutes, to 15 hours and 27 minutes (London)

1 hour and 22 minutes, to 16 hours and 6 minutes (Glasgow)

Cloud types

Altocumulus

Cirrus

Cumulonimbus

Cirrocumulus

stratus

cumulus

THE SEA

Average sea temperature

Orkney:	12.9°C
Scarborough:	15°C
Blackpool:	15.8°C
Brighton:	15.4°C
Penzance:	16.5°C

Spring and neap tides

The spring tide is the most extreme tide of the month, with the highest rises and falls, and the neap tide is the least extreme, with the smallest. Exact timings vary around the coast, but expect each around the following dates:

Spring tides:	14th–15th and 28th–29th
Neap tides:	7th–8th and 20th–21st

Dolphins and whales

Between June and October is a good time to try to catch a glimpse of some of the mega fauna that resides in or takes a summer migration through the seas around our coast, all making the most of our rich sea life while the weather is good and the sea is at its warmest. Hotspots include Lyme Bay, Cardigan Bay, Anglesey, Llŷn Peninsula and the Sarnau, Celtic Deep, Pembrokeshire Marine, Bideford Point, the Lizard, Manacles, Silver Pit and Farnes East. Visit for glimpses of minke whales, fin whales, humpback whales, bottlenose dolphins, common dolphins, white-beaked dolphins, harbour porpoises and basking sharks.

THE GARDEN

Planting by the moon

Full moon to 3rd quarter: 1st–6th. Harvest crops for immediate eating. Harvest fruit.

3rd quarter to new moon: 6th–13th. Prune. Harvest for storage. Fertilise and mulch the soil.

New moon to 1st quarter: 13th–19th. Sow crops that develop below ground. Dig the soil.

1st quarter to full moon: 19th–27th. Sow crops that develop above ground. Plant seedlings and young plants.

Full moon to 3rd quarter: 27th–31st. Harvest crops for immediate eating. Harvest fruit.

Jobs in the garden
- Move your houseplants out of doors for the summer. Give the leaves a dust and a shower, then give the roots a feed and a good soaking, and they will quickly look twice the plants they were.
- Give hanging-basket plants a trim to encourage them to bush up. Feed once a week and water once a day.
- Strawberry plants will have thrown out 'runners' by now. Pin them onto the surface of pots of compost and keep them well watered, and they will root there and can later be severed from the main plant and used to plant up a new strawberry bed, or given away.

Glut of the month – courgette
The courgette glut is the glut of all gluts. The word 'glut' in the dictionary should just be a picture of a courgette, or seven. This is the month.
- You can stem the tide of courgettes by picking them when they are very tiny or even when they are still flowers. Courgette flowers are delicacies, with a sweet and vegetable-like crunch, and tiny courgettes are denser and sweeter than

big ones. Eat both raw, or lightly fried in butter and finished with lemon juice and salt.

- Courgette fritters. Grate a couple of courgettes into a tea towel and then wrap and squeeze out the excess moisture. Tip into a bowl and mix in half a packet of feta, one beaten egg, and a couple of tablespoons of plain flour. Fry spoonfuls of the mixture in hot oil.
- Roughly chop several courgettes and drop into a saucepan with good extra virgin olive oil, crushed garlic, pepper and salt. Cook slow and covered until they are soft enough to crush with a fork. Squeeze over the juice of half a lemon and serve as a side dish, warm or cold.

Garden task – sow again

Typically we make a frenzy of sowings in early summer and then sit back and watch everything grow, which leads to a wonderful heap of produce and flowers in July and August but little beyond. Sowing now will extend the season into autumn, winter and next spring, and it is easy when the ground is warm and seeds can be sown direct. There are a few different types of sowings to be made now for future colour, fragrance and crops.

- Late-summer vegetables. Sow short rows of spinach, lettuce, rocket, beetroot, radishes and spring onions every few weeks. Make a final sowing of courgettes, French beans and peas now for when yours run out of steam.
- Biennial flowers. These are plants that need to grow through one season to flower the next, and they include some of the best and most fragrant cut flowers: sow honesty, foxgloves, sweet William, sweet rocket and night-scented stock in nursery beds now.
- Autumn vegetables. Sow rows of Oriental greens mibuna, mitsuna, pak choi and others for autumn now. Sow your last batch of beetroot, plus fennel.
- Winter and spring vegetables. It is too late to start Brussels sprouts, winter cabbages and autumn cauliflowers, but you can buy and plant plug plants. Sow autumn cabbages now, and winter carrots and turnips.

KITCHEN

In season

- This is the start of the fruit bonanza. **Apricots, peaches** and **nectarines, cherries, raspberries, currants, gooseberries, blueberries** and **strawberries** are all in season. The first **plums, blackberries, tayberries** and **loganberries** are ripening.

- Garden veg is bounteous. **New potatoes,** young **carrots, salads, peas, asparagus, globe artichokes, mangetout, spring onions, lettuce, runner beans, French beans, celery** and **rocket** are all ready, and **courgettes** are producing almost daily. There may be a few **broad beans** around but this is the end of their season.

- Make use of the summer herbs that are at their best now, in particular **mint, basil** and **dill.** Edible flowers will be in bloom on the vegetable patch, including **courgette flower** and **nasturtium.**

- **Sea bass, mackerel, sardines** and **crab** are all plentiful.

- All of the fresh, young cheeses are wonderful at the moment as milk is produced from animals on plentiful, fresh grass.

Ingredient of the month – green walnuts

Green walnuts are those picked before they have formed a shell, and they have been eaten pickled since at least the eighteenth century. Looking like shiny, deepest-brown marbles, and tasting both sweet and sour, pickled walnuts are eaten with blue cheese at Christmas. First, catch your green walnuts. They are good for this in July only, so go foraging or track down supplies on the internet. Take 2 kg of green walnuts and prick each with a fork, then put them in a bowl, cover with water, and tip in 225 g salt. Leave for a week, then drain and repeat. Drain and leave the walnuts out to dry for a few days, during which time they will turn black. Slowly heat 1 l of malt vinegar with 500 g sugar, 1 tsp each of cloves, allspice berries and black peppercorns, and a cinnamon stick until the sugar has dissolved, then add the walnuts and boil for 15 minutes. Spoon walnuts and liquid into jars and seal.

RECIPES

Vegetables à *la Française*

This is a useful recipe to have up your sleeve for when you have a bucketful of green vegetables and want a good way to use them up. It is traditionally *petit pois à la Française*, but the name change is just to let you know that you can throw in any green vegetables that are weighing heavily on your mind. Serve it as a vegetable side dish or as lunch with a hunk of bread and some good cheese.

Ingredients

3 spring onions

2 cloves garlic

50 g butter

1 Little Gem lettuce

150 ml hot chicken or vegetable stock (use water if you don't have the real thing)

300 g peas/French beans/runner beans/mangetout/shelled broad beans or a mixture of several

Salt and pepper

Method

Chop the spring onions and garlic and cook them in the butter until they are soft. Shred the lettuce and add it to the pan, stirring until it has wilted. Add the stock or water, bring to the boil and add the vegetables. Simmer with the lid off until all is cooked and tender but still vibrant and green. Season and serve.

Sundowners

'Sundowner' is a term from Britain's colonial past, denoting a long, cool drink served in a highball glass and taken at sunset – an icy and alcoholic breather between a long hot day and dinner. Gin and tonic is the classic sundowner, and here are three others:

- **Lime Rickey:** fill a glass with ice cubes, pour in 2 oz gin and a squeeze of lime juice. Top up with club soda and stir, garnishing with a wedge of lime.
- **Mint julep:** muddle together 3 oz bourbon, 6 sprigs of mint and 2 tbsp of simple syrup in the bottom of a glass, crushing the mint. Add ice, then top up with club soda, stir, and garnish with a mint leaf.
- **Moscow mule:** fill a glass with ice and pour on 1 ½ oz vodka and 1 oz lime juice, then top up with ginger beer, stir and garnish with a lime wedge.

J

NATURE

Look out for:

- Hedgerows full of nettles, burdock, cleavers, creeping thistle, meadow crane's-bill. The wild clematis known at this stage of its life as traveller's joy (and later as old man's beard) is draped over the hedgerows, flowering brightly.
- In shadier spots and in the north foxgloves are just coming into flower. Meadowsweet flowers in ditches and on damp verges.
- Red and white clover flower in bee-friendly, neglected lawns. Rosebay willowherb bursts into flower across disturbed ground. Pineappleweed flowers along rough paths.
- Buddleia, the butterfly bush, comes into flower, and will be covered in basking and pollen-sipping red admirals, small tortoiseshells, peacock, chalkhill, marbled white and common blue butterflies, and buzzing with bees.
- Towards the end of the month grass flower heads start to mature and turn golden and straw-coloured. Meadows may have been cut by now, or at the very least will be starting to shed seed.
- Look out for red poppies and white campion along the edges of arable fields.
- On chalk and limestone grasslands look for fragrant orchids, pyramidal orchids and common spotted orchids. Also harebell, marjoram, thyme, field scabious and greater knapweed.
- Adult cuckoos leave our shores this month for Africa, the first of the summer migrants to depart. Their offspring follow later.
- Swarms of low-flying summer insects can lead to spectacular swooping displays from swifts, swallows and house martins.

Crop circles

July is the month in which the most crop circles appear, stems trampled, bent or otherwise transformed into beautiful geometric patterns within golden fields. The earliest known report of a crop circle was in 1678 in Hertfordshire, but it was the 1970s that saw the start of a resurgence of circles that has now become a boom, with 40–50 appearing every summer, and sometimes more.

Most crop-circle activity is concentrated in Wiltshire, a county blessed with a combination of large, flat arable fields – this month filled with wheat and barley tall enough to take a pattern, but not yet ready to be harvested – and mysterious, prehistoric monuments. Crop circles are often found in the vicinity of Stonehenge and Avebury and the smaller prehistoric sites around them. Famous hoaxers Bower and Chorley have claimed responsibility for a great many crop circles since they went public in 1991, and some are now claimed by other crop-circle artists, who have steadily grown in number and whose methods and ideas have become increasingly sophisticated and ambitious.

Crop circles nowadays are no mere circles – they are grand and intricate works of art, often representing complex mathematical formulas or astronomical patterns. Of course not everyone thinks that all are manmade, and those who want to believe have many convincing arguments that something more mysterious and complex is afoot than a couple of blokes with a measuring tape and a plank. Either way, Honeystreet, a small village roughly equidistant between the two big sites, has become unofficial crop circle HQ, and sees a great influx of circle-spotters each summer. Some come to stand in the rippling fields simply to admire this blossoming and seasonal guerrilla art form, some to commune with a sense of wonder, possibility and cosmic mystery.

August

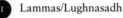

- **1** Lammas/Lughnasadh
- **3** 3rd–27th: Edinburgh Festival
- **6** Summer bank holiday (Scotland)
- **12** The 'Glorious Twelfth' (start of grouse shooting season in England, Scotland and Wales)
- **22** Eid al-Adha (Muslim celebration)
- **26** Raksha Bandhan (Hindu celebration)
- **26** 26th–27th: Notting Hill Carnival
- **27** Summer bank holiday (England, Wales, Northern Ireland, Guernsey)

Home in August takes on a deliciously doldrums-like quality. If you are able to take time off then days spill into each other in a haze of nothing much, maybe an afternoon visit to a lido with the papers one day, a dusk potter in the garden with a frosted glass of wine the next. If you are at work in August then the most basic task feels like wading through treacle, with every other email met instantly by an out-of-office reply that whispers: *I am elsewhere, lying in dappled shade with a book, gasping as a cold, sun-sparkling wave crashes over me. Your sales figures will wait.*

There is a suspension of activity and expectation in August, and it is good to see how little we can get away with. We have worked hard and now we can reap some time. But into the space that August leaves we do pour fun: holidays by the sea, barbecues with people we mean to spend more time with but never do, festivals, carnivals and day trips. There is another kind of reaping to be done too, as all of the produce of the vegetable patch, the cut-flower garden and the hedgerow start to ripen at once. In the countryside there is a sense of summer waning. The colours are turning slowly away from green towards golden, and in hot weather the grasses start to look parched and tired. A switch has been thrown: growth is no longer the goal, it is all about ripening now. All of this is a sign that these languid days will not last forever. Enjoy your August, you've worked hard for it.

THE SKY

Moon phases

3rd quarter – 4th August

New moon – 11th August

1st quarter – 18th August

Full moon – 28th August

In the night sky this month

13th	The Perseid meteor shower peaks tonight and will have no interference from moonlight. The radiant will appear 43 degrees above north-eastern horizon at midnight, though you may get more of a show towards dawn.
17th	Close approach of moon with Jupiter tonight, visible briefly at dusk, 15 degrees above the south-western horizon.
21st	Close approach of moon with Saturn tonight, highest at 10 p.m., 15 degrees above the southern horizon.

A

Constellation of the month – Pegasus

Look to the east in the early evening and you will be able to pick out the 'square of Pegasus', the most easily identified part of the constellation, formed by four particularly bright stars. The square makes up the body of the winged horse. Scheat is the brightest of these four stars and is a red giant about 200 light years away from earth. It is almost 100 times larger in diameter than our sun. The square of Pegasus is a useful tool in determining sky-watching conditions: if you can pick out more than eight stars within its borders, you have a good dark sky; any fewer and light pollution is preventing you from seeing the sky at its best.

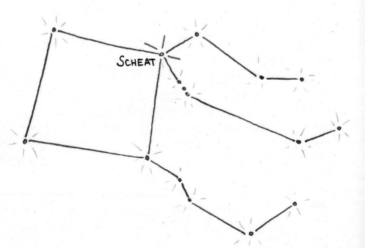

Moon rise and set

	London		Glasgow		
	Rise	Set	Rise	Set	
1st	22.57	10.02	23.16	10.15	
2nd	23.18	11.09	23.33	11.27	
3rd	12.19	23.41	23.51	12.41	
4th	–	13.30	–	13.56	3rd quarter
5th	00.06	14.43	00.12	15.14	
6th	00.35	15.58	00.37	16.33	
7th	01.12	17.11	01.10	17.49	
8th	01.58	18.19	01.53	18.59	
9th	02.56	19.19	02.50	19.57	
10th	04.06	20.08	04.02	20.43	
11th	05.24	20.47	05.24	21.18	new moon
12th	06.47	21.20	06.51	21.46	
13th	08.09	21.47	08.19	22.09	
14th	09.29	22.12	09.44	22.29	
15th	10.47	22.36	11.06	22.48	
16th	12.01	23.00	12.25	23.08	
17th	13.12	23.25	13.41	23.29	
18th	14.21	23.53	14.54	23.54	1st quarter
19th	15.26	–	16.02	–	
20th	16.26	00.26	17.05	00.23	
21st	17.21	01.04	18.01	00.59	
22nd	18.09	01.49	18.48	01.43	
23rd	18.50	02.40	19.27	02.34	
24th	19.24	03.36	19.59	03.33	
25th	19.54	04.37	20.25	04.37	
26th	20.19	05.41	20.47	05.45	full moon
27th	20.42	06.47	21.05	06.55	
28th	21.03	07.54	21.23	08.06	
29th	21.24	09.01	21.40	09.18	
30th	21.46	10.10	21.57	10.31	
31st	22.09	11.20	22.17	11.45	

A

Moon watching

Train a birdwatching telescope or even a pair of binoculars on the moon and suddenly it leaps into three dimensions, the white disc printed becoming a solid sphere with weight and heft, improbably suspended. Although we love to gaze at the moon when it is full, it's not the best time to take a closer look. It is too glaring. The sun is shining straight onto every nook and cranny so there are no shadows, making features harder to pick out. The best time of the month is either at or just after the 1st quarter phase (which falls this month on the 18th), or at or just before the 3rd quarter (the 4th). Then the moon is half full, the sun shines on it from one or the other side, and every mountain range and valley along the lunar sunrise/sunset line is perfectly picked out.

WEATHER

We long for heat waves and the long and languid dog days in August, but while temperatures are dependably warm, August is most often characterised by drama, with the energy of heat and humidity building into towering cumulonimbus clouds that release thunder, lightning and torrential rain. In early summer, thunderstorms are brief, but by August they have turned into prolonged downpours, and in large parts of the east August is routinely the wettest month of the year (not to suggest that the west gets away lightly: this is only because the west is so much wetter the rest of the time). Should a wondrous heat wave manifest – and occasionally they do – enjoy it for the outlier it is.

Average temperatures (°C):	London 19, Glasgow 15
Average sunshine hours per day:	London 6, Glasgow 5
Average days rainfall:	London 13, Glasgow 21
Average rainfall total (mm):	London 48, Glasgow 60

Day length

During the course of August, day length decreases by:

1 hour and 46 minutes, to 13 hours and 38 minutes (London)

2 hours and 8 minutes, to 13 hours and 54 minutes (Glasgow)

THE SEA

Average sea temperature

Orkney:	13.2°C
Scarborough:	15.6°C
Blackpool:	16.7°C
Brighton:	16.9°C
Penzance:	17.1°C

Spring and neap tides

The spring tide is the most extreme tide of the month, with the highest rises and falls, and the neap tide is the least extreme, with the smallest. Exact timings vary around the coast, but expect each around the following dates:

Spring tides:	12th–13th and 27th–28th
Neap tides:	5th–6th and 20th–21st

Rock-pooling

August is the month most of us are most likely to find ourselves poking at limpid pools with bright pink plastic nets, forcing crabs, shrimp and tiny fish to scurry out from seaweed hideaways. When the sea recedes it leaves behind these glimpses of what was previously mysterious and hidden beneath the waves. Each rock pool is its own world, with its own host of temporary and longer-term inhabitants, but the nature of the pool will vary according to its position on the shore. The upper seashore is only covered during spring tides, and pools there can be full of gutweed and no good for rock-pooling. The middle shore takes the fiercest battering of waves, and here you will find lots of limpets and barnacles. The best pools for rock-pooling will be on the lower seashore, those only uncovered during the lowest tides. Look out for blennies and gobies, little fish that skulk under rocks, and for anemones, starfish and crabs.

Rock pool inhabitants

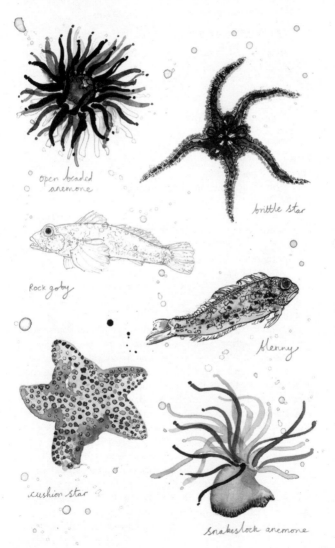

open beaded
anemone

brittle star

Rock goby

blenny

cushion star ?

snakeslock anemone

A

Sunrise and set

| | *London* | | *Glasgow* | |
	Rise	Set	Rise	Set
1st	05.24	20.49	05.21	21.24
2nd	05.26	20.57	05.23	21.22
3rd	05.27	20.45	05.25	21.20
4th	05.29	20.44	05.27	21.18
5th	05.30	20.42	05.29	21.16
6th	05.32	20.40	05.31	21.14
7th	05.33	20.38	05.33	21.11
8th	05.35	20.37	05.35	21.09
9th	05.36	20.35	05.37	21.07
10th	05.38	20.33	05.38	21.05
11th	05.39	20.31	05.40	21.03
12th	05.41	20.29	05.42	21.00
13th	05.43	20.27	05.44	20.58
14th	05.44	20.25	05.46	20.56
15th	05.46	20.23	05.48	20.53
16th	05.47	20.21	05.50	20.51
17th	05.49	20.19	05.52	20.49
18th	05.51	20.17	05.54	20.46
19th	05.52	20.15	05.56	20.44
20th	05.54	20.13	05.58	20.41
21st	05.55	20.11	06.00	20.39
22nd	05.57	20.09	06.02	20.37
23rd	05.58	20.07	06.04	20.34
24th	06.00	20.05	06.06	20.32
25th	06.02	20.02	06.08	20.29
26th	06.03	20.00	06.10	20.27
27th	06.05	19.58	06.12	20.24
28th	06.06	19.56	06.14	20.22
29th	06.08	19.54	06.15	20.19
30th	06.10	19.52	06.17	20.17
31st	06.11	19.49	06.19	20.14

THE GARDEN

Planting by the moon

Full moon to 3rd quarter: 1st–4th. Harvest crops for immediate eating. Harvest fruit.

3rd quarter to new moon: 4th–11th. Prune. Harvest for storage. Fertilise and mulch the soil.

New moon to 1st quarter: 11th–18th. Sow crops that develop below ground. Dig the soil.

1st quarter to full moon: 18th–26th. Sow crops that develop above ground. Plant seedlings and young plants.

Full moon to 3rd quarter: 27th–31st. Harvest crops for immediate eating. Harvest fruit.

Jobs in the garden

- When off on your holidays, group your pots together in a shady place, and stand them in trays of water. Do the same with houseplants, either indoors or out: it is warm enough for them to be outside, but the bath makes a handy water tray.
- Harvesting is the main job at the allotment, so leave plenty of time for it and do it regularly and frequently. There is a huge difference between a French bean picked when sweet, tender and tiny and one that should have been picked a week ago, and that difference is the thing that makes growing your own worthwhile.
- Potato blight can devastate crops very quickly and arrives in late summer in warm and wet weather. Look out for rotting or shrivelling leaves and brown blotches on the stems. Dig up and use any affected crops as soon as possible, or cut off the leaves and earth up the stems to try to prevent further damage to the potatoes.

A

Glut of the month – sweetcorn

The sugars in sweetcorn quickly start to turn to starch once it is cut, so whatever you do with yours, do it quickly. Really fresh sweetcorn is one of the perks of the gardener's year.

- Leave the husks on and throw them onto the barbecues until they are burnt, then peel back to reveal bright-yellow cooked kernels with a smoky flavouring. Slather in butter and sprinkle with salt.
- Make a flavoured butter to lather over by mixing additions with softened butter: chive and garlic; chilli and lime zest; basil and Parmesan; caramelised onion and sundried tomato. Make ahead and store in the fridge.
- Southern US-style corn is boiled in a pot of water with a half-pint of milk, a good pinch of salt, and 125 g butter added to the pot. No need to add butter when it comes out.

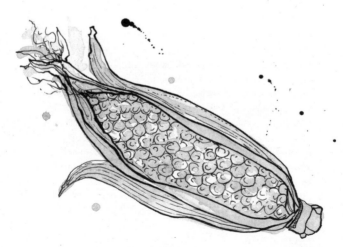

Garden task – sow green manures

Green manures are sold as big packets of seed to be sown directly on to fallow earth. There they germinate and grow quickly and thickly, covering the soil. There are several purposes to sowing a green manure. The main point is to create bulky organic matter that can be dug into the soil to improve its structure: a great solution if you want to give your soil a treat but don't have access to farmyard manure or lots of compost, or if you don't have adequate strength or stamina to hump that stuff around. They also drag up nutrients from the soil and make them more easily available to your plants: some have deep roots that go down, search the goodness out, and then hold it captive in the leaves until it can be released into the top soil to be grabbed by hungry vegetables such as courgettes and winter squash. Green manures also germinate so thickly across the soil that they prevent weeds from getting a toehold. And finally, those sown in August and September will cover the soil all winter, protecting it from rains that might wash topsoil away and leach nutrients.

The green manures to sow now and dig in during spring are:

- **Winter tares.** An annual, fast-growing vetch that fixes nitrogen. After you dig it into the soil in spring, plant with nitrogen-lovers such as leafy vegetables.
- **Winter field bean.** Another nitrogen-fixer, and particularly good on heavy soils and soils that need breaking up. It is a legume, so do not plant peas or beans straight after it.
- **Grazing rye.** Deep roots and a good nutrient-fixer, and can be used anywhere in a vegetable garden's rotation. Very hardy and continues to grow in cold weather.

FESTIVITIES

Lammas

The festival of Lammas is the first harvest festival, and a celebration of early August. And what a fine moment it is: all bounty and ripening warmth, deep blue skies and wheeling swifts. Like Imbolc, Beltane and Samhain, Lammas was one of the Celts' 'cross-quarter' days: the dates that fall between the solstices and the equinoxes and that were used to mark out the agricultural year. This one marks the wheat harvest, and the arrival of the first berries. The wheat and barley have ripened and can be brought in, and the berries are fat and black on the bramble bushes. This would have been a time of hard work and good rewards, of grafting in teams in the fields to bring in the harvest by day, and enjoying the first breads and beers of the new crop by night.

In Anglo-Saxon manuscripts Lammas is often referred to as the 'feast of the first fruits', and the word comes from the Anglo-Saxon *hlaf-mas* (loaf mass). On Lammastide a loaf of bread made from the new crop would be brought in to church to be blessed, and then the loaf was thought to have taken on protective qualities. Now the harvesting methods have changed, but the cycle remains the same, and this is the time you will see combine harvesters carving their massive swathes through hazy fields (and you will get stuck behind them as they trundle dustily between neighbouring farms on narrow country roads). It is a day to appreciate the turning of the year and the bounty and fun that it eventually brings, and to celebrate your own hard work and harvest.

KITCHEN

In season

- **Plums** are at their best this month. Summer-fruiting **raspberries** finish now, but autumn-fruiting varieties begin. The first **figs** and **melons** start to ripen. Other fruits this month: **blackcurrants, redcurrants, tayberries, apricots, peaches, blueberries,** early-ripening **apples** and **pears**.
- Late-summer treats are starting to ripen: **sweetcorn, tomatoes, sweet peppers, chilli peppers** and **aubergines** join **courgettes, carrots, fennel, French** and **runner beans, potatoes, beetroot, lettuce, sorrel, spinach, cucumbers** and **radish**. Herbs are plentiful.
- Look out for **cobnuts**, picked when green, unripe and crunchy. In the hedgerows look out for **elderberries** and **crab apples**, just starting to ripen. **Sea buckthorn** is fruiting.
- **Plaice, mackerel, sardines, megrim sole, squid, crab, lobster** and **scallops** are all in season.
- **Goat meat** is available all year round, but it is particularly good and cheap this month, as increased production is timed to coincide with carnival season and with Eid al-Adha.

Ingredient of the month – brambles

Call them blackberries if you like, but there is something special about the word 'bramble', covering as it does both the fruit itself and the act of gathering them. To bramble is to ramble and search, to take on the thicket, sleeves resolutely down, and to cover yourself in scratches and deep purple splodges anyway. You can buy blackberries or grow them in the garden, but it is not only the experience that will be missed: wild blackberries have a complexity of flavour that is completely lacking in the cultivated types, a wild, woodsy, homely taste, nostalgia in berry form. That is, if you get them fully ripe, not sharp and mean, and the way to spot these best few is to look for a fat, black shine that the unripe berries just don't have. Pick them, then look at the inside: if this is still white then the berry is underripe and should be taken home for heat and sugar, ideally mixed with apples in the best crumble filling combination; if it is purple it can be popped straight into your mouth.

A

RECIPES

Bramble babka

A special loaf for a glorious moment in the year, this takes a
little doing, but make it ahead of time and take it up to the
allotment around Lammas time to keep you well fuelled while
harvesting, and to toast the arrival of the berries and the wheat.

Ingredients
For the dough
125 ml whole milk
10 g instant yeast
75 g sugar
500 g strong white bread flour
1 tsp salt
3 eggs, lightly beaten
150 g butter, softened
For the filling
500 g blackberries
225 g sugar
1 piece of star anise
For the glaze
3 tbsp of the blackberry mixture
A little water

Method

Heat the milk in a pan until it is warm to the touch but not
hot. Stir in the yeast and a pinch of sugar and let the mixture
sit for 5 minutes, or until the surface is foamy. Mix the flour,
salt and remaining sugar in a large bowl. Make a well in the

centre and pour in the yeasty milk and the eggs, mixing with a wooden spoon at first and later your hands to bring it into a dough. Work the softened butter in, a little at a time. (If you have a mixer with a large bowl and a dough hook, you can put all of these ingredients in together and mix until you have a smooth dough, about 8 minutes.) Tip the dough into a clean bowl, cover with cling film and leave to prove in the fridge overnight. For the filling, wash the blackberries, then heat gently with the sugar and star anise until the sugar has dissolved and the juices have been released. Simmer and stir for around 10 minutes until thick and jammy. Leave to cool. (You will have plenty of this left over after making the recipe, but it can be used as jam, stored in a jar in the fridge for several weeks.)

Take two loaf tins, 22 cm x 10 cm, oil them and line with parchment. Knock back the dough, split it into two equal-sized pieces, and roll each out on a well-floured surface to around 40 cm square. Spread a layer of the blackberry jam mixture over each and roll them up tightly. Take one roll and slice it down the centre, then lay these two pieces alongside each other, cut sides facing upwards. 'Spiral' the two pieces around each other, always keeping the cut sides facing upwards. Pinch together the ends, then fold and twist the whole thing back on itself once. Pinch the ends together and tuck underneath the roll, then slot it into one of the loaf tins. Repeat with the other roll. Cover with a tea towel and leave to prove for about 2 hours, or until the loaves have doubled in size.

Preheat your oven to 180°C/350°F/gas mark 4. Bake for 35–40 minutes. Make the glaze by warming a little jam in a pan with a splash of water. Either paint it onto the freshly baked loaves, lumps and all, or sieve first. Leave the babkas to cool for 10 minutes before tipping out and cooling completely on a wire rack.

Curry goat A recipe by Natasha Miles

The end of August brings Notting Hill Carnival, the biggest street carnival in Europe and a celebration of the heritage and culture of the British West Indian community. One of the most popular dishes at Carnival is curry goat, served from food stalls, a vibrant and rich dish that no Jamaican party or celebration is complete without. Its spicy flavours dance on the tongue to the beat of the parade. The use of Scotch bonnet pepper is what sets this dish apart: it has a sweet aromatic flavour but a fiery temper, and can deliver a tremendous punch of heat if not treated with respect and kept whole throughout the cooking. Betapac curry powder is a Jamaican brand with a high proportion of turmeric, while Bolst's has a richer spice blend. You can find both in Indian food shops, but if not, then use a standard curry powder.

Serves 5

Ingredients

1 $^{1}/_{3}$ kg goat shoulder
2 medium onions
1 tbsp Betapac curry powder (or curry powder of your choice)
1 tbsp Bolst's curry powder (or curry powder of your choice)
2 tbsp vegetable oil
3 cloves crushed garlic
1 chopped carrot
1 scotch bonnet pepper
2 sprigs of thyme
1 heaped tsp pimento seeds
Salt and pepper to taste

Method

Place the meat in a mixing bowl, slice one of the onions and place over the meat, then add both of the curry powders. Mix thoroughly, cover the bowl with cling film and refrigerate for 12 hours, or overnight.

Take the meat out of the fridge and rest for 30 minutes before cooking. Scrape the onion off the meat and set aside. In a large pan add the oil and heat to a high temperature, then add the meat and half of the other onion, sliced. Fry vigorously until all the meat is brown, then reduce heat to a very low temperature and cover with a lid to slowly simmer. The meat will steam and create its own juices. After 30 minutes of cooking add the garlic, carrot, whole scotch bonnet pepper (do not chop it up), the reserved onions and the rest of the other onion, thyme, pimento seeds and salt and pepper to taste. Cook for 3–4 hours, or until the meat is tender. After 2 hours of cooking, carefully fish out the pepper, whole, or if you like your curry really hot, leave it in. If the sauce starts to dry out at any point, top it up it with water, but not too much, as you don't want to dilute the flavours. Serve with white basmati rice.

A

NATURE

Look out for:
- Blackberries, elderberries, hawthorns and sloes start to ripen, and both birds and foragers move in to feast.
- Heathland heathers are now flowering and covering hillsides with purple. Bilberries are ready to pick.
- Hot days bring the sound of grasshoppers stridulating from long grass, advertising their territories to mates.
- Meadow brown butterflies, small skipper butterflies, large white butterflies and gatekeeper butterflies.
- Estuaries start to fill as waders return there after breeding or to prepare for migration. Look out for bar-tailed godwits, golden plovers and lapwings.
- Lords and ladies are fruiting at the base of hedgerows.
- Riverbanks are pretty with the flowers of meadowsweet, purple loosestrife and great willowherb.
- Garden birds can look a little rough this month as they slowly moult and replace their feathers. Remember to provide water for bathing and drinking.
- Most swifts fly south this month.

Flying-ant day

In July or August there falls a day when suddenly we are
plagued by flying ants, the biblical atmosphere compounded
by the packs of seagulls that wheel overhead to feast on them.
This is flying-ant day, brief, impressive and not particularly
beautiful, but essential to the ant life cycle. There is no
signal to take to the skies – the ants respond to weather cues,
generally flying when a period of wet weather is followed by a
period of warm and dry conditions, and so you may see flying
ants over several days, culminating in one impressive day. They
mate on the wing, the females coming back to earth to create
a new colony over which to preside for the rest of their earth-
bound year.

A

September

- **1** Start of meteorological autumn
- **10** Rosh Hashanah (Jewish new year)
- **10** Start of Muharram (Islamic new year)
- **12** Start of Ganesh Chaturthi (Hindu festival celebrating the birth of Ganesh)
- **19** Yom Kippur (Jewish holiday)
- **23** Autumnal equinox
- **23** Start of astronomical autumn
- **23** Mabon (pagan celebration)
- **29** Michaelmas Day

If you want a resolution to stick, make it in September. There is a new-broom feel about September, a sense that it is time to stop mucking about and to get down to business. There is historical precedent for this feeling, a sort of administrative shaking down that came with the completion of the harvest, and with the ending of long, warm days and the advent of colder, darker ones. If summer must end, and if we must go back to school, let's do so with crisp white shirts, polished shoes, a brand new pencil case and some serious good intentions.

The Anglo-Saxons called September Haligmonath, holy month, or the month of offerings to give thanks for the harvest. Harvesting, bottling and preserving are still in full swing for a little while at least. Going back to school in September can feel cruel, as the weather is often surprisingly calm and summery. Gold is slowly becoming the predominant colour: in the fields; on the first of the trees; in the harvest moon, hanging low, large and yellow in the sky. But despite the lazy feel to the countryside this is a naturally busy time: preparing for hibernation isn't easy. There is work to be done.

THE SKY

Moon phases

3rd quarter – 3rd September

New moon – 9th September

1st quarter – 17th September

Full moon – 25th September

In the night sky this month

| 17th | Close approach of the moon with Saturn tonight, from around 8.30 p.m., 15 degrees above the southern horizon. |
| 20th | Close approach of the moon and Mars tonight, at its highest at 9.30 p.m., 14 degrees above the southern horizon. |

S

Constellation of the month – Cygnus

Cygnus, the Swan, is one of the constellations in the Summer Triangle, its brightest star, Deneb, forming one of the three points. But even though summer is slipping away, elegant Cygnus can be seen high in the sky up close to the zenith at around 11 p.m. In fact, if you know where to look – low in the east in the morning sky in spring, and low in the west in the evening sky in autumn – you can find it year round. Deneb means 'tail', and Sadr, the name of the star at the centre of the constellation, means 'breast'. Albireo, a binary star of contrasting orange and blue hues, is the 'Beak Star'. It is well worth looking at through good binoculars.

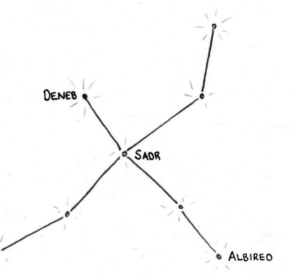

Moon rise and set

	London		Glasgow		
	Rise	Set	Rise	Set	
1st	22.36	12.32	22.40	13.01	
2nd	23.09	13.45	23.09	14.18	
3rd	23.05	14.56	23.46	15.34	3rd quarter
4th	–	16.05	–	16.44	
5th	00.41	17.06	00.35	17.46	
6th	01.44	17.58	01.39	18.35	
7th	02.57	18.41	02.54	19.14	
8th	04.16	19.16	04.18	19.44	
9th	05.39	19.45	05.46	20.09	new moon
10th	07.01	20.11	07.13	20.31	
11th	08.21	20.36	08.31	20.50	
12th	09.38	21.00	10.00	21.10	
13th	10.53	21.25	11.20	21.31	
14th	12.05	21.52	12.36	21.54	
15th	13.14	22.24	13.49	22.22	
16th	14.17	23.00	14.55	22.56	
17th	15.15	23.43	15.55	23.37	1st quarter
18th	16.05	–	16.46	–	
19th	16.49	00.32	17.28	00.26	
20th	17.25	01.27	18.01	01.23	
21st	17.56	02.27	18.29	02.25	
22nd	18.23	03.30	18.52	03.32	
23rd	18.46	04.35	19.11	04.42	
24th	19.08	05.42	19.29	05.53	
25th	19.29	06.51	19.46	07.06	full moon
26th	19.50	08.00	20.03	08.20	
27th	20.13	09.11	20.22	09.35	
28th	20.39	10.23	20.44	10.52	
29th	21.10	11.36	21.10	12.09	
30th	20.48	12.49	21.44	13.25	

S

WEATHER

The 1st of September marks the start of meteorological autumn, and the days noticeably begin to shorten following the autumnal equinox on the 23rd. But September is often surprisingly beautiful and can put summer to shame, only deteriorating into rainy weather later in the month. The thundery showers of summer are in decline as temperatures drop, and the autumnal and wintery westerlies that bring wet weather from across the Atlantic are strengthening, but sometimes there is a little golden spell in between. Nights can be long enough for mists to form, particularly towards the end of the month, and the first gales of autumn – equinoctial gales – can arrive, the remnants of Atlantic and Caribbean hurricanes.

Average temperatures (°C):	London 17, Glasgow 13
Average sunshine hours per day:	London 5, Glasgow 4
Average days rainfall:	London 15, Glasgow 20
Average rainfall total (mm):	London 49, Glasgow 80

Day length

During the course of September, day length decreases by:

1 hour and 53 minutes, to 11 hours and 41 minutes (London)
2 hours and 13 minutes, to 11 hours and 37 minutes (Glasgow)

On the autumnal equinox on the 23rd, night and day are the same length. It is one of only two days a year (the other being the vernal equinox in March) when the sun rises precisely due east and sets due west.

Sunrise and set

	London		*Glasgow*	
	Rise	Set	Rise	Set
1st	06.13	19.47	06.21	20.11
2nd	06.14	19.45	06.23	20.09
3rd	06.16	19.43	06.25	20.06
4th	06.18	19.40	06.27	20.04
5th	06.19	19.38	06.29	20.01
6th	06.21	19.36	06.31	19.58
7th	06.22	19.34	06.33	19.56
8th	06.24	19.31	06.35	19.53
9th	06.26	19.29	06.37	19.51
10th	06.27	19.27	06.39	19.48
11th	06.29	19.24	06.41	19.45
12th	06.30	19.22	06.43	19.43
13th	06.32	19.20	06.45	19.40
14th	06.34	19.18	06.46	19.37
15th	06.35	19.15	06.48	19.35
16th	06.37	19.13	06.50	19.32
17th	06.38	19.11	06.52	19.30
18th	06.40	19.08	06.54	19.27
19th	06.42	19.06	06.56	19.24
20th	06.43	19.04	06.58	19.22
21st	06.45	19.01	07.00	19.19
22nd	06.46	18.59	07.02	19.16
23rd	06.48	18.57	07.04	19.14
24th	06.50	18.55	07.06	19.11
25th	06.51	18.52	07.08	19.08
26th	06.53	18.50	07.10	19.06
27th	06.54	18.48	07.12	19.03
28th	06.56	18.45	07.14	19.00
29th	06.58	18.43	07.16	18.58
30th	06.59	18.41	07.18	18.55

S

THE SEA

Average sea temperature

Orkney:	12.9°C
Scarborough:	14.9°C
Blackpool:	16.1°C
Brighton:	17.3°C
Penzance:	16.5°C

Spring and neap tides

The spring tide is the most extreme tide of the month, with the highest rises and falls, and the neap tide is the least extreme, with the smallest. Exact timings vary around the coast, but expect each around the following dates:

Spring tides:	10th–11th and 26th–27th
Neap tides:	4th–5th and 18th–19th

Estuary birds

In early autumn the bird population of estuaries swells as birds arrive from the continent and take advantage of the insect-rich mudflats. This is an excellent time of year to visit estuaries for birdwatching. Visit at high tide, when the birds are pushed into smaller areas of mudflat closer to the shore. Take binoculars and look out for oystercatchers, godwits and redshanks.

THE GARDEN

Planting by the moon

Full moon to 3rd quarter: 1st–3rd. Harvest crops for immediate eating. Harvest fruit.

3rd quarter to new moon: 3rd–9th. Prune. Harvest for storage. Fertilise and mulch the soil.

New moon to 1st quarter: 9th–17th. Sow crops that develop below ground. Dig the soil.

1st quarter to full moon: 17th–25th. Sow crops that develop above ground. Plant seedlings and young plants.

Full moon to 3rd quarter: 25th–30th. Harvest crops for immediate eating. Harvest fruit.

Jobs in the garden

- Keep camellias and rhododendrons well watered as they are forming next spring's flower buds and will drop them or make fewer if their roots are dry.
- Tip mints out of pots and loosen a few of the white roots spiralling around the outside. Snip these off and lay them on the surface of a pot of compost and cover lightly. Keep watered, and you will soon have new plants to grow on your windowsill in winter when outdoor plants have died down.
- Time for ripening tomatoes is running out. Count four trusses of tomatoes on each plant and cut off any above this, or six if you are growing in a greenhouse or polytunnel, then cut away leaves that are shading remaining fruits.

S

Glut of the month – damsons

These rich and sour little plum-like fruits arrive all at once
in great quantity in hedgerows and in gardens, and will spoil
after just a few days sitting around in buckets and bags in the
kitchen. Be ready with the preserving kit.

- Damsons make the very best jam of the year, rich and sharp
  in flavour and deep purple in colour. Wash 1 ½ kg damsons
  and place in a pan with 450 ml water. Bring to the boil and
  simmer for 30 minutes, pushing the fruits against the edge
  occasionally to loosen flesh from stone. Fish out the stones
  as they rise to the surface (resign yourself to not getting
  them all), add 1 ⁴/₅ kg sugar, heat gently and stir until
  dissolved, then boil until the temperature reaches 105°C.
  Cool slightly, pour into sterilised jars, and seal.

- Make damson cheese, our native equivalent to membrillo, a
  sliceable preserve to serve with cheese. Slowly simmer 2 kg
  damsons with a splash of water until they are completely
  soft, then rub through a sieve or colander to remove the
  stones and skins. For every 500 ml of puree add 350 g
  sugar and then simmer and stir for up to an hour until the
  mixture thickens enough that you can briefly draw a clear
  line along the bottom of the pan. Pour into oiled plastic
  containers to set.

- Small bottles of damson vodka make excellent Christmas
  presents. Fill a large Kilner jar with 1 kg damsons, 500 g
  sugar and 1 l vodka. Seal and put away, revisiting it to shake
  it occasionally. It will be ready by Christmas, or even better
  by the following one.

Garden task – force bulbs for Christmas

You can plant bulbs every couple of weeks throughout winter, but here is the timetable to hit Christmas:

- **15th–29th September:** Prepared hyacinths. Most need around 10 weeks in the cool and dark and then three weeks in the light. (Note: some varieties need less time than this; check when buying and count back from Christmas day.) Bring them out of the gloom when the shoots are a few centimetres tall and you can see the embryonic flower within.

- **15th October–13th November:** Hippeastrum bulbs. They do not need a period of chilling or of dark. Pot them into small pots, half the bulb above the soil level. Place on a cool, sunny windowsill and turn as they grow.

- **27th November–11th December:** Paperwhites. The easiest and quickest of the lot, with beautifully scented, pale cream-coloured flowers. Pot up, water and grow on a sunny windowsill.

S

KITCHEN

In season

There are so many vegetables in season this month. All of the Mediterranean vegetables are at their best now: tomatoes and aubergines are reaching their brief and delicious glut, and chillies are ripe and ready for picking. Runner beans, French beans, cucumbers, sweetcorn, beetroot, broccoli, carrots, salad leaves, maincrop potatoes, and more are ready. Turnips, leeks, kale and other autumn/winter crops are starting to come in too. There is an embarrassment of riches.

- Fruits of the months include **plums, blackberries, apples, pears** and autumn **raspberries. Figs** are now ripe and juicy, and there are plenty of **melons, nectarines** and **peaches** to be had. In the hedgerow look for **damsons, elderberries** and **blackberries.**
- **Cobnuts** can be picked or bought while still green and fresh.
- Herbs are plentiful, including **parsley, oregano, thyme, basil** and **coriander.**
- **Grouse, partridge, duck, goose** and **guinea fowl** are coming into season.
- **Crab, scallops, lobster, hake, megrim sole, sardines, mackerel** and **plaice** are all abundant.

Chilli types

scotch bonnet

JALEPENO

banana pepper

birds eye

ALEPPO

POBLANO

Ingredient of the month – goose
It was once as common to eat goose on Michaelmas Day as it now is to eat turkey at Christmas. Birds were hatched in spring, raised all summer, and turned out to graze and fatten up on the stubble of the fields once the harvest was in, and so they became inextricably linked to the Michaelmas end-of-harvest celebrations. The custom fell out of favour as fewer lives were linked so closely to the harvest, but there has been a small resurgence in the tradition of the Michaelmas goose in recent years, and it is certainly at its best now. The meat is something halfway between white chicken meat and red meat, far richer and more flavourful than chicken or turkey. The fat, too, is packed with flavour and makes the very best roast potatoes. Nowadays many geese are raised in factory farming conditions, so take care to source a free-range, organic bird or one that has been hunted in the wild. The goose-hunting season begins on 1st September and ends on 31st January.

FESTIVITIES

Michaelmas, Muharram and Rosh Hashanah: September as new year

The 29th of September, Michaelmas Day, once acted as a kind of administrative new year in Britain: annual rents were due, annual employment terms expired, and new mayors elected. It is still the date upon which the Lord Mayor of London is elected each year (a post that has existed since 1192, as opposed to the post of the Mayor of London, created in 2000). Local courts would be held and new school terms began, the children that had been needed to help with the harvest finally released. Michaelmas Day was a day for pomp and ceremony, sorting, paperwork and new beginnings.

The Islamic New Year, Muharram, begins this month, some Muslims celebrating it on the 10th of the month every year and others when it is ushered in by the new moon, this year on the 12th. This month is also one of four Jewish new years. Rosh Hashanah is the new year for people, animals and for legal contracts. It can fall any time between 5th September and 5th October, occurring this year on 10th September. As well as being the start of the economic year – again, likely tied to the end of the harvest originally – it involves a more spiritual kind of account-keeping, a period of self-examination and repentance. On Rosh Hashanah God opens the Book of Life and the Book of the Dead, 10 days of prayers and repentance follow, and then on Yom Kippur the judgement is sealed. A traditional greeting on Rosh Hashanah is *Ketivah VaChatimah Tovah,* 'a good inscription and sealing'.

There is a prevailing wind of fresh starts, self-reflection and renewed productivity in September, of admin for self-improvement. Catch it if you can. It is the time to take out newly sharpened pencils and brand new stationery, to look at the achievements and failures of the year past, set them aside, then start work on new ideas and new plans.

S

RECIPES

Chutney

Chutney is one of many Indian foods that became absorbed into British cuisine during and following colonisation. And like other Indian foods, chutney underwent a transformation as it travelled. In India chutney is a freshly made spicy and savoury relish served at the side of a dish; here it means a cupboard preserve of vegetables or fruits slow-cooked in spices, vinegar and sugar. Far less healthy than the original perhaps, but an essential recipe to have under your belt to deal with the gluts of September, and to keep you in cheese and pickle sandwiches for the rest of the year.

The basic chutney ratio is 12:4:2 of produce:vinegar:sugar, so for instance 3 kg fruits and vegetables, 1 l malt vinegar, 500 g sugar, as below. You can reduce the amount of sugar if using mainly fruits, and reduce the amount of vinegar if using very acidic produce such as tomatoes.

Ingredients

3 kg vegetables, chopped to a roughly uniform size (include some apples and some onions as a rule, and some sultanas if you like them)

500 g soft brown sugar

2 tsp salt

1 l malt vinegar

1½ cm fresh ginger, grated

A piece of muslin, tied around: 1 tsp mustard seeds, 1 tsp allspice berries, a few coriander seeds, 1 bay leaf, half a cinnamon stick, two whole cloves

Method

Put all of the ingredients into a large preserving pan, bring to the boil, then simmer for around two hours, stirring frequently, until the vegetables are soft and the consistency is thick, and a wooden spoon drawn across the base of the pan briefly leaves a clear line. Remove the muslin, pour the chutney into sterilised jars, and seal. Leave to mature for several months before using.

Imam biyaldi – Swooning imam

Aubergines are ripe and perhaps even in glut if you have been a good gardener. So make the most of them. In this luxurious Turkish dish, aubergine is lavished with the two things it loves best: good olive oil and time. Vegetables cooked this way are known as *zeytinyağlı* (with olive oil), and eaten at room temperature with plenty of bread to soak up the oil and juices, perfect for a late-summer lunch.

Serves 2
Ingredients
2 aubergines
9 tbsp extra virgin olive oil
2 onions, finely sliced
6 garlic cloves, sliced
1 tin chopped tomatoes
1 tsp paprika
2 tbsp pomegranate molasses
Salt and pepper
Fresh mint, chopped

S

Method

Slice the aubergines in half lengthways, leaving the imam's 'hat' in place. Scoop out a length of the inside of each half, dice, and set aside for later. Heat 2 tbsp of the olive oil in a frying pan and fry the halves of aubergine on each side for several minutes, until they start to soften, then set them aside. Put a couple more tablespoons of oil into the pan and fry the chopped aubergine with the onion. After about 5 minutes add the garlic, then cook all until softened. Add the tomatoes, paprika and pomegranate molasses and simmer together for 5 minutes, then add salt and pepper to taste. Jigsaw the aubergines together, cut side up, in a frying pan and fill the cavities with the sauce. Pour 100 ml of water and the rest of the olive oil (about 5 tbsp) into the pan and bring it to the boil, then turn the heat down low and cover with a lid or kitchen foil. Simmer for around 45 minutes. The aubergines should be slippery-soft. The flavours improve if this dish is left to sit and meld, so eat later, cold or at room temperature, sprinkled with the mint.

NATURE

Look out for:

- Perennial plants begin to die down to their roots. Seed heads are now the most beautiful things in the garden, though late-flowering garden plants become an important source of pollen for bees and butterflies. Ivy begins to flower now and will provide into winter.

- Trees and shrubs start to give hints of autumn colour. Ash, beech, sweet chestnut and horse chestnut are among the first to show colour changes. Sycamore and maple seeds helicopter to the ground and conkers start to fall.

- Hips and haws take over from flowers in the hedgerows, and sloes, blackberries and elder are ripening all the time.

- Wasps become problematic. They have been around all year, but in late summer their queen stops giving them sweet rewards for their work, and so they come hunting for jam sandwiches and lemonade. Crane flies, better known as daddy longlegs, appear in September too.

- This is the start of the mushroom season. Look out for giant puffballs in fields, which when young and fresh are delicious sliced and fried in butter.

- Food is plentiful for birds at the moment, but it is a good idea to start feeding this month, so that they know where to find it when it is scarce.

- This is a huge month for bird movements, as many summer migrants set off for warmer places. Estuaries and mudflats act as stopping-off points.

- Hedgehogs are feeding themselves up ahead of hibernation. Put out food (dog food isn't bad; milk and bread are terrible) and leave lots of twigs, dead leaves and debris in the garden.

- Gatekeeper butterflies, common blue butterflies and speckled wood butterflies are still around.

S

October

For much of October we can play at autumn. We get golden sunlight, tapestry-like hillsides, morning mists, all without any great drop in temperature: a gentle slide into everything good about autumn. We light the fire because we can, because it's October, not because we are so cold that we have to. The countryside is ravishing, and ripening before our eyes, every hedgerow glistening with lipstick-red hips and purple elderberries, hazelnuts and walnuts and glossy sweet chestnuts in their hedgehog casings, every tree a different shade. The year's spiders are now fully grown, and are suddenly everywhere, stretching their webs over hedges and across the garden path, the fine strands breaking across your face each morning.

Gather in nuts and logs and final crops, because towards the end of the month things start to feel more serious. Frosts arrive and the clocks go back, and we remember what this ripening is all about. The Anglo-Saxons called this month Winterfylleth, a word composed of 'winter' and 'full moon', and they thought that winter began on October's full moon, which falls this year on the 24th. Prematurely pessimistic, perhaps, but night and cold are slowly becoming dominant.

THE SKY

Moon phases

3rd quarter – 2nd October

New moon – 9th October

1st quarter – 16th October

Full moon – 24th October

3rd quarter – 31st October

In the night sky this month

15th	Close approach of moon with Saturn tonight, visible after dusk, 14 degrees above southern horizon.
18th	Close approach of moon and Mars tonight, highest at 8.15 p.m., 18 degrees above southern horizon.
21st & 22nd	Orionids meteor shower, the dust from Halley's Comet, radiant from the area above Orion. The nearly full moon means only the brightest tracks will be visible.
26th	Venus changes from being an evening planet to a morning planet, but will be lost in the glare of the sun for the next few weeks.

O

Constellation of the month – Andromeda

Attached to the great square of Pegasus – starting the evening in the east and rising up to the zenith by 11 p.m. – is Andromeda. It is named after the mythical princess and daughter of Cassiopeia, whose zigzag-shaped constellation is nearby. Its brightest star, Alpha Andromedae, is a binary star that is also often considered part of Pegasus. On a clear night without too much light pollution you should be able to pick out a misty spot just above Andromeda with the naked eye, and certainly through binoculars. This is the Andromeda Galaxy, which has been estimated to contain a trillion stars, around twice as many as our Milky Way. The Milky Way and Andromeda galaxies are expected to collide in 4.5 billion years, eventually merging together to form a giant galaxy.

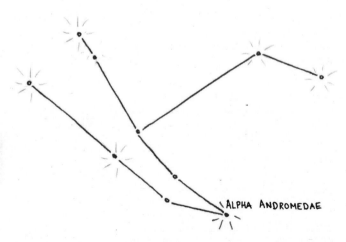

Moon rise and set

	London		Glasgow		
	Rise	Set	Rise	Set	
1st	22.34	13.48	22.29	14.37	
2nd	23.32	15.00	23.26	15.40	3rd quarter
3rd	–	15.53	–	16.32	
4th	00.39	16.38	00.35	17.13	
5th	01.54	17.14	01.54	17.45	
6th	03.13	17.45	03.18	18.11	
7th	04.34	18.11	04.44	18.33	
8th	05.54	18.35	06.09	18.52	
9th	07.13	18.59	07.32	19.12	new moon
10th	08.30	19.24	08.54	19.32	
11th	09.44	19.50	10.14	19.54	
12th	10.56	20.20	11.30	20.20	
13th	12.04	20.55	12.41	20.51	
14th	13.05	21.35	13.45	21.29	
15th	14.00	22.22	14.41	22.16	
16th	14.46	23.15	15.26	23.10	1st quarter
17th	15.26	–	16.03	–	
18th	15.58	00.14	16.33	00.11	
19th	16.26	01.16	16.57	01.16	
20th	16.50	02.20	17.17	02.25	
21st	17.12	03.27	17.35	03.36	
22nd	17.33	04.35	17.52	04.48	
23rd	17.45	05.45	18.09	06.02	
24th	18.16	05.45	18.27	07.18	full moon
25th	18.16	08.10	18.47	08.36	
26th	19.10	09.24	19.12	09.56	
27th	19.46	10.39	19.44	11.15	
28th	19.30	10.51	19.25	11.30	
29th	20.25	11.57	20.18	12.37	
30th	21.29	12.53	21.24	13.33	
31st	22.41	13.40	22.39	14.17	3rd quarter

O

WEATHER

Like September, October can bring glorious reminders of summer as winds come in from the south, with only misty mornings and dark evenings hinting that change is coming. By the end of the month the sun travels to only just over 30 degrees above the horizon, which means that its light reaches us through a greater slice of atmosphere than it does at midsummer, accounting for its rich and golden hue. October can also be highly tempestuous and stormy, with wintery storms quickly moving in and closing down any thoughts of a lingering Indian summer. Frosts often appear on higher ground in northern areas at the beginning of the month, and creep into more central areas by the end of the month.

Average temperatures (°C):	London 13, Glasgow 10
Average sunshine hours per day:	London 3, Glasgow 3
Average days rainfall:	London 15, Glasgow 24
Average rainfall total (mm):	London 71, Glasgow 110

Day length
During the course of October, day length decreases by:

1 hour and 54 minutes, to 9 hours and 54 minutes (London)

2 hours and 14 minutes, to 9 hours and 18 minutes (Glasgow)

Sunrise and set

| | London | | Glasgow | |
	Rise	Set	Rise	Set
1st	07.01	18.38	07.20	18.53
2nd	07.03	18.36	07.22	18.50
3rd	07.04	18.34	07.24	18.47
4th	07.06	18.32	07.26	18.45
5th	07.07	18.29	07.28	18.42
6th	07.09	18.27	07.30	18.40
7th	07.11	18.25	07.32	18.37
8th	07.12	18.23	07.34	18.34
9th	07.14	18.21	07.36	18.32
10th	07.16	18.18	07.38	18.29
11th	07.17	18.16	07.40	18.27
12th	07.19	18.14	07.42	18.24
13th	07.21	18.12	07.44	18.22
14th	07.23	18.10	07.46	18.19
15th	07.24	18.07	07.48	18.17
16th	07.26	18.05	07.50	18.14
17th	07.28	18.03	07.52	18.12
18th	07.29	18.01	07.54	18.09
19th	07.31	17.59	07.56	18.07
20th	07.33	17.57	07.58	18.05
21st	07.35	17.55	08.00	18.02
22nd	07.36	17.53	08.02	18.00
23rd	07.38	17.51	08.04	17.57
24th	07.40	17.49	08.06	17.55
25th	07.41	17.47	08.08	17.53
26th	07.43	17.45	08.11	17.50
27th	07.45	17.43	08.13	17.48
28th*	06.47	16.41	07.15	16.46
29th	06.49	16.39	07.17	16.44
30th	06.50	16.37	07.19	16.41
31st	06.52	16.35	07.21	16.39

Note: on the 28th this chart switches from British Summer Time to Greenwich Mean Time.

THE SEA

Average sea temperature

Orkney:	12°C
Scarborough:	12.7°C
Blackpool:	14.4°C
Brighton:	16.3°C
Penzance:	14.8°C

Spring and neap tides

The spring tide is the most extreme tide of the month, with the highest rises and falls, and the neap tide is the least extreme, with the smallest. Exact timings vary around the coast, but expect each around the following dates:

Spring tides:	10th–11th and 25th–26th
Neap tides:	3rd–4th and 17th–18th

THE GARDEN

Planting by the moon

3rd quarter to new moon: 2nd–9th. Prune. Harvest for storage. Fertilise and mulch the soil.

New moon to 1st quarter: 9th–16th. Sow crops that develop below ground. Dig the soil.

1st quarter to full moon: 16th–24th. Sow crops that develop above ground. Plant seedlings and young plants.

Full moon to 3rd quarter: 24th–31st. Harvest crops for immediate eating. Harvest fruit.

Jobs in the garden
- Collect up fallen leaves and stuff them into their own compost bin or perforated bin bags, then water and forget them. In a year or two you will have crumbly leaf mould.
- Frosts are coming. Put away any tender plants that you want to survive winter. Pelargoniums, succulents and aeoniums all need a cool, bright and frost-free place: a porch, a cool spare room, or a slightly heated greenhouse.
- Plant spring bulbs. Get daffodils in as soon as possible, and crocuses, scillas, fritillaries and muscari not long after.

Glut of the month – winter squash and pumpkins
Get winter squash and pumpkins in ahead of the frosts. Cure the skins somewhere dry and sunny and they will store well.
- Sweet and sour treatment lends winter squash some welcome sharpness. Heat 1 tbsp of caster sugar with 2 tbsp of vinegar until syrupy, then pour over roasted squash pieces and top with chilli flakes, or with feta, toasted walnuts and mint.
- Bake pieces of winter squash in a big tray with whole tomatoes, quartered onions, and a packet of thick sausages.
- You will make squash soup, there is no escaping it. Enliven it with a topping of crispy fried onions, strips of bacon, slivers of Parmesan or toasted pumpkin seeds, or all four.

O

Garden task – save your lawn

Your lawn looks awful after a summer of children and dogs trampling it, or drought, or flooding, or just plain old neglect. We don't pay much attention to our lawns, but they carry on serving us faithfully anyway, providing a carpet on which to walk barefoot and roll about in the summer, and a square of vivid green to gaze upon when all else is brown in winter. With very little trouble it can be beautiful next summer: soft and springy and with all bare patches sprouting green again.

In October the ground is warm from a summer of heat and moist from autumn rains. Grass seeds germinate easily, and while colder weather soon comes along and stops top growth, the roots keep on growing and spreading all autumn and winter, creating a strong foundation from which new growth can spring when the weather warms next year.

For a full autumnal lawn service you will need: a spring-tine rake; your mower; a garden fork; sharp sand and compost, mixed half and half; a hard-bristled brush; grass seed; some pieces of horticultural fleece and some tent pegs. Start by energetically going over the whole lawn with the rake, scratching out dead grass and moss from the roots. Now mow, and remove the clippings. Push your garden fork straight down into the ground at intervals of about a foot, as deep as you can, then brush in the sand and compost (particularly do this on compacted areas such as by the gate and goal mouths). Finally, scratch at the surface of the bare patches and sow thickly with seed. Water well and pin over a piece of horticultural fleece or fine net to keep the birds off, just until the seed germinates. The lawn will look truly awful – its very worst – but it will rise, phoenix-like, next spring.

KITCHEN

In season
There are still plenty of greenhouse veg around – aubergines,
tomatoes and chillies – though their season is drawing to
a close as colder weather arrives. The more unusual root
vegetables of the year are now ready: salsify, scorzonera and
Jerusalem artichokes, as well as there being plenty of beetroots,
carrots and parsnips around. Brassicas move into prime
position, and there will be kale and cabbage no matter what the
weather does.

- This is wild mushroom season. Look for **ceps, chanterelles**
  and **puffballs** in specialist delis. **White truffles** are in season.
- There is a great abundance of tree fruit in October: **apples,
  pears, quinces, medlars. Grapes** are maturing and you can
  still find the last **figs** and **blackberries**.
- It is hunting season, and you may find **duck, goose, grouse,
  guinea fowl, hare, pheasant, rabbit** and **venison** in specialist
  butchers.
- This is the end of the **mackerel** season. There is plenty of
  hake, lemon sole and **sardines. Oysters** are back in season.

Ingredient of the month – apples to store
Some apples – particularly the earliest maturing varieties – are
flighty things, built for eating within a few days, but declining
in quality beyond that. Others mature and develop in storage.
This slow ripening process gives some of the finest and most
complex flavours. They are well worth waiting for: keepers, if
you like. Choose and plant long-storing varieties and you could
still be eating your own apples at wassailing time and beyond.
'Ashmead's Kernel' develops pear drop and citrus undertones
as it matures, and is good for eating or cider making; 'Cornish
Gillyflower' is a Victorian variety which slowly takes on a
rich, sweet, clove-like fragrance; 'Sturmer Pippin' can be left
hanging on the tree until January, and is at its best in February
or March, when it is sweet and crisp. Eat the windfalls now
as they will not store, but pick and wrap the best of the crop
individually in newspaper, and store until you need them.

O

RECISPES

Crumble blueprint

It is crumble season. This is a recipe you can use for apples now, but can also adapt all year round for whatever fruit you have in abundance. Almost every element of it is changeable, and swapping the type of flour, sugar or rubble can make this an entirely different dessert. Muck about. It does for between 500–700 g fruit, either placed in the pie dish raw with the juice of half a lemon and a couple of tablespoons of sugar, or pre-cooked (for harder fruits such as apples and quince).

Ingredients
75 g butter
100 g flour/ground almonds
75 g sugar
100 g rubbly stuff: rolled oats, chopped nuts
2 tsp spice/zest

Method
Rub the butter into the flour or ground almonds until it resembles rough breadcrumbs, then stir in the sugar, rubble and spice. Sprinkle it over the fruit, pat it down lightly, then bake for 30–45 minutes at 190°C/375°F/gas mark 5.

Some variations:

- Apple and sultana filling with wholemeal flour, oats, cinnamon, light soft brown sugar and pecan topping
- Pear and quince filling with spelt flour, muscovado sugar, ground clove and chopped walnut topping
- Rhubarb filling with demerara sugar, ground ginger, chopped stem ginger and orange zest topping
- Plum filling with wholemeal flour, ground almonds, sliced almonds and golden caster sugar topping
- Apricot, strawberry and vanilla filling with white flour, oats, caster sugar and lemon zest topping

And so on...

O

Apple brandy hot toddy

To warm you up on the long evenings.

Makes 2
Ingredients
360 ml cider
1 tsp honey
1 stick cinnamon
1 lemon
100 ml apple brandy or Calvados

Method
Divide the apple brandy between two heatproof glasses or
mugs, then take two slices from the lemon and drop one into
each. Heat the cider, honey, cinnamon and the juice of the rest
of the lemon in a small saucepan for a few minutes, then pour
it over the apple brandy and drink while hot.

A brief history of time changing

This month brings the most brutal manifestation of our homogenised time keeping. We know we are slipping towards winter but the abrupt end of British Summer Time makes the descent almost shocking, like a curtain dropping. Time wasn't always mucked about with like this; it was simply what the sun said it was. Solar noon moved across the country, east to west, so Norwich was several minutes ahead of London, Oxford five minutes behind it, Leeds six minutes behind, Bristol ten minutes behind, and so on, with town clocks across the country all displaying their own local time. It was the railways that changed all of this. With their quick journey times between time zones, almanacs had to be printed alongside timetables to avoid accidents and allow passengers to make connections, but the potential for problems was huge. Slowly but surely through the 1800s each of the railways gradually adopted London time. In 1880 the unified standard time for Great Britain was made law.

So, relatively speaking, the country's time had only recently been brought into line when the idea arose to change it for summer. Perhaps it was the realisation that time can be played with, and bent to our own convenience, but in 1905 William Willett began campaigning for the hour change to allow for greater enjoyment of summer evening hours. British Summer Time was finally introduced in 1916, a year after his death. This is the moment in the year when we stop playing and revert back to something closer to the true astronomical time – give or take ten minutes or so – and we do feel the difference. Raise a glass of something autumnal and warming in memory of Willett, and of all those stolen summer hours, to ease the pain.

NATURE

Look out for:

- Blackberries are all but over, but hazelnuts are ripening, if you can beat the squirrels to them. Look out for forageable walnut trees and sweet chestnut trees in parks and parkland, and take a bucket. Sloes are prominent and easy to pick now, but they are at their best after the first frost.
- In damp weather this is prime month for fungi. Go on a woodland hunt, but do not pick to eat unless you are with an expert.
- In the Scottish Highlands and across some of England's national parks, the red deer rut is underway.
- Birds are almost silent now with the exception of robins, which sing their melancholy song as they begin staking out and protecting next year's territory.
- House martins have flown away by the end of October. Redwings and fieldfares arrive from Scandinavia and make use of the berries in countryside hedges.

Autumn colour

Autumn colour is reaching its peak towards the end of the month, as deciduous trees gradually stop producing the green chlorophyll that helps them to produce food from sunlight, and close down for the winter. The absence of chlorophyll reveals a different colour in every tree. Beech forests turn a beautiful warm copper, and birch forests buttery yellow. In forests dominated by one species even the air seems to take on a glow. Hedgerows turn a patchwork of yellow field maple, brown hazel, and yellow wych elm. A few species, including some of the more spectacular coloured Japanese maples that fill arboretums and gardens, are often at their best in November, blustery storms willing.

Common spiders

FALSE WIDOW SPIDER

cellar spider

cardinal

ZEBRA JUMPING SPIDER

giant house spider

LACE WEB SPIDER

O

189

November

1   All Saints' Day

1   Samhain (pagan celebration day)

2   All Souls' Day

3   Bridgwater Carnival

5   Guy Fawkes Night

7   Diwali (the Hindu, Sikh and Jain festival of lights)

11   Remembrance Sunday

12   Martinmas

21   Prophet's Birthday (Muslim celebration day)

25   Stir-up Sunday

30   St Andrew's Day (local holiday, Scotland)

November is the month in which we fight the encroaching dark with light: Guy Fawkes Night, Samhain, Diwali, all November festivals centred around light, sparks and fire. A drift of wood smoke and the occasional tang of sulphur is the scent of November. All of these festivals have a secondary focus on sweet treats – Bonfire Night parkin, cinder toffee and toffee apples; soul cakes at Samhain; Diwali sweets – as if our ancestors knew that the fire battles were all very well, but the true way to make it through winter is by comfort eating.

The old Anglo-Saxon name for the month was Blotmonath, blood month, as this was the traditional time to slaughter animals and preserve meat, to save the expense of having to keep animals alive through winter, and to make the most of a summer and autumn of fattening up. The slaughter also lent itself to hearty feasting, as those parts that could not be preserved were cooked up. This has always been a bountiful month, despite and because of the increasing cold.

It can also be a beautiful month, as the fiery final trees flame with colour in the pale sunlight, or it can be as bare as January if a big storm has blown all the last leaves away. After a storm we see the stems for the first time: purples, oranges, yellows and whites. Old man's beard seed heads open now to reveal the fluffy insides that give them their name, and caught by low winter sunlight they look like strings of fairy lights hung out across the nearly bare hedgerows. It is a month for finding warmth, and light, wherever you can find it.

THE SKY

Moon phases

New moon – 7th November	
1st quarter – 15th November	
Full moon – 23rd November	
3rd quarter – 30th November	

In the night sky this month

5th & 6th	Taurids meteor shower (Northern), a low rate of meteors but there is no moon and so a good, dark sky for spotting. The radiant is overhead.
11th	Close approach of the crescent moon with Saturn tonight, from dusk, 12 degrees above the southern horizon.
12th	Taurids meteor shower (Southern), with the radiant 60 degrees above the southern horizon. The moon sets early for good spotting.
16th	Close approach of the moon and Mars tonight, after dusk, highest at 6.30 p.m., 25 degrees above the southern horizon.
17th & 18th	Leonids meteor shower, a low rate of meteors but a good dark sky after midnight. The radiant is low over the east–northeast horizon.

N

Constellation of the month – Taurus and the Pleiades

In November look for Taurus, the Bull, located by its brightest star Aldebaran, which begins the night low in the east, is high overhead at midnight, and moving to low in the western sky just before dawn. As night falls look straight up from Aldebaran and you should find the beautiful star cluster of the Pleiades, also in Taurus. The Pleiades is known as the Seven Sisters for the stars it contains, most of which are blue and highly luminous. It is one of the closest star clusters to earth and the one most visible to the naked eye. The return of the Pleiades to the northern sky in September heralded the beginning of autumn, but now it is at its most beautiful and visible. The two Taurid meteor showers can be seen this month, radiating from the constellation. This was originally one shower, which has been split into two by gravitational effects over time.

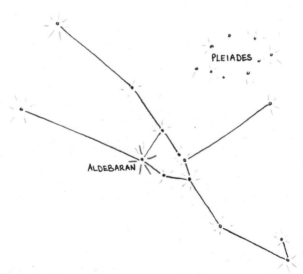

Moon rise and set

	London		Glasgow		
	Rise	Set	Rise	Set	
1st	23.58	14.17	–	14.50	
2nd	–	14.48	00.01	15.16	
3rd	01.16	15.15	01.24	15.38	
4th	02.34	15.39	02.47	15.58	
5th	03.52	16.01	04.09	16.16	
6th	05.08	16.25	05.30	16.34	
7th	06.23	16.49	06.50	16.55	new moon
8th	07.37	17.17	08.08	17.18	
9th	08.47	17.49	09.23	17.47	
10th	09.52	18.27	10.31	18.22	
11th	10.51	19.12	11.32	19.05	
12th	11.42	20.03	12.23	19.56	
13th	12.24	21.00	13.03	20.55	
14th	13.00	22.01	13.36	21.59	
15th	13.29	23.04	14.02	23.07	1st quarter
16th	13.54	–	14.23	–	
17th	14.16	00.09	14.41	00.16	
18th	14.37	01.16	14.58	01.27	
19th	14.58	02.24	15.14	02.40	
20th	15.19	03.35	15.31	03.55	
21st	15.42	04.48	15.50	05.12	
22nd	16.09	06.03	16.12	06.32	
23rd	16.42	07.20	16.41	07.54	full moon
24th	17.23	08.36	17.19	09.14	
25th	18.15	09.47	18.08	10.28	
26th	19.18	10.49	19.12	11.30	
27th	20.29	11.40	20.26	12.19	
28th	21.46	12.21	21.47	12.55	
29th	23.01	12.54	23.10	13.24	
30th	–	13.21	–	13.46	3rd quarter

N

WEATHER

There are generally three types of November weather: the gloomy and grey, the stormy, and the occasional gloriously sunny, when you can stride around woodlands or arboretums enjoying the autumn colours before one of those stormy days comes along and blows it all away. Since the late 1800s the number of sunshine hours in each day in November has steadily increased, partly due to the decrease in smog-forming fuels in cities, but also because the pattern of November winds has slowly changed from a predominance of cloudy southerlies to increased clear and cold northerlies. And so we are now far more likely to have a few glorious autumnal days than we were a century ago.

Average temperatures (°c):	London 10, Glasgow 6
Average sunshine hours per day:	London 2, Glasgow 2
Average days rainfall:	London 17, Glasgow 24
Average rainfall total (mm):	London 63, Glasgow 100

Day length

During the course of November, day length decreases by:

1 hour and 36 minutes, to 8 hours and 13 minutes (London)
1 hour and 45 minutes, to 7 hours and 28 minutes (Glasgow)

Sunrise and set

	London		Glasgow	
	Rise	Set	Rise	Set
1st	06.54	16.34	07.23	16.37
2nd	06.56	16.32	07.25	16.35
3rd	06.57	16.30	07.27	16.33
4th	06.59	16.28	07.30	16.31
5th	07.01	16.27	07.32	16.29
6th	07.03	16.25	07.34	16.27
7th	07.04	16.23	07.36	16.25
8th	07.06	16.22	07.38	16.23
9th	07.08	16.20	07.40	16.21
10th	07.10	16.19	07.42	16.19
11th	07.11	16.17	07.44	16.17
12th	07.13	16.16	07.46	16.15
13th	07.15	16.14	07.49	16.13
14th	07.17	16.13	07.51	16.12
15th	07.18	16.11	07.53	16.10
16th	07.20	16.10	07.55	16.08
17th	07.22	16.09	07.57	16.07
18th	07.23	16.07	07.59	16.05
19th	07.25	16.06	08.01	16.03
20th	07.27	16.05	08.03	16.02
21st	07.28	16.04	08.05	16.00
22nd	07.30	16.03	08.07	15.59
23rd	07.32	16.02	08.09	15.58
24th	07.33	16.01	08.10	15.56
25th	07.35	16.00	08.12	15.55
26th	07.36	15.59	08.14	15.54
27th	07.38	15.58	08.16	15.53
28th	07.39	15.57	08.18	15.52
29th	07.41	15.56	08.19	15.51
30th	07.42	15.56	08.21	15.50

N

THE SEA

Average sea temperature

Orkney:	10.9°C
Scarborough:	10.6°C
Blackpool:	12.3°C
Brighton:	14.7°C
Penzance:	13.2°C

Spring and neap tides

The spring tide is the most extreme tide of the month, with the highest rises and falls, and the neap tide is the least extreme, with the smallest. Exact timings vary around the coast, but expect each around the following dates:

Spring tides:	8th–9th and 24th–25th
Neap tides:	1st–2nd and 16th–17th

Grey seal pupping

Grey seals all around the coastline give birth to their pups between November and January. Just under half the world's population of this beautiful mammal live around our shores, and this is the only time that they come to shore for extended periods, and so is a good time to spot them. Keep your distance, and look at them through binoculars, and if you are lucky you will see a still-fluffy pup before it turns sleek and seaworthy, basking on a beach or rocky outcrop with its mother. Cornwall, Lincolnshire, Northumberland, Norfolk, Pembrokeshire, the Outer Hebrides and the Orkneys are prime areas.

THE GARDEN

Planting by the moon

3rd quarter to new moon: 1st–7th. Prune. Harvest for storage. Fertilise and mulch the soil.

New moon to 1st quarter: 7th–15th. Sow crops that develop below ground. Dig the soil.

1st quarter to full moon: 15th–23rd. Sow crops that develop above ground. Plant seedlings and young plants.

Full moon to 3rd quarter: 23rd–30th. Harvest crops for immediate eating. Harvest fruit.

Jobs in the garden

- Feed the birds. There is still plenty of natural food in the hedgerows and gardens, but start feeding now so they know where to come in leaner times. Choose high-fat foods to help them through cold nights: peanuts, grated cheese and suet, fat balls.
- Plant up a pot or a hanging basket with winter bedding: pack violas and pansies in close as they won't grow much.
- Buy little terracotta pot feet to lift your containers a couple centimetres or so from the ground and stop them getting waterlogged over winter.

N

Glut of the month – borlotti beans

Collect your borlotti beans, pop them out of their pods and dry them properly so that they will store well. Simmer fresh borlotti beans for 25–30 minutes. Once dried they need to be soaked overnight, then boiled hard in lots of water for 10 minutes, and then simmered for a further 1–2 hours, until they are completely soft.

- Alternatively you can boil dried borlottis just covered in water topped up with a generous glug or several of extra virgin olive oil, plenty of fresh sage, some cloves of garlic and a couple of tomatoes. Simmer long and slow until cooked through and you will just need to add a little seasoning and some vinegar and they are ready to eat.
- *Pasta e fagioli* is a classic Italian borlotti and pasta soup. Cook a diced onion, carrot and stalk of celery in 4 tbsp of extra virgin olive oil until they soften. Add 250 g uncooked soaked or fresh beans with enough water to cover the beans by 5 cm, plus a deseeded and chopped chilli and a sprig of rosemary. Cook until the beans are soft (up to 2 hours) then add 1 tbsp of tomato puree, salt and pepper to taste, and 150 g small pasta. The soup is ready when the pasta is ready.
- Make into a spread for bruschetta by blending cooked borlotti beans with a little plain yoghurt, plenty of grated Parmesan, basil leaves, salt and pepper and extra virgin olive oil.

Garden task – plant tulips

Tulips are wonderfully forgiving of the tardy gardener, as they need to be planted late in the year, well after all of the other bulbs. There is zero skill needed to create an amazing late-spring display with them: all the hard work in building up the bulb has been done for you by the bulb grower, and all you have to do is pop them into the ground. Plant tulip bulbs at three times their own depth, in pots or in the soil. Here are some ways to plant them.

- Alongside wallflowers. This is an old-fashioned combination but is a classic for a reason, as wallflowers are planted at the same time (find them as bare-root plants in garden centres now), flower at the same time, and create a fuzz of flowers for grandly tulips to rise up through.
- Dot them in among existing shrubs and perennials. This can work really beautifully, particularly where young plant growth is emerging, and where you have pretty and frothy spring plants such as forget-me-not and *Alchemilla mollis*.
- Mass them together in pots or – if you are feeling really flash – along pathway edges. You need to use plenty to do this approach justice: big and bold. The benefit with pots is that you can fling them into centre stage when they are looking perfect, then tuck them out of sight as they fade.
- Naturalise species types in grass for a jewelled lawn. Red *Tulipa spengeri* and yellow *Tulipa sylvestris* are the ones to try, in a patch of sunny grass.

N

KITCHEN

In season

We are down to the hardiest of garden vegetables now:
Jerusalem artichokes, carrots, beetroot, leeks, parsnips,
cauliflower, Brussels sprouts, kale, winter cabbage, stored
maincrop potatoes, borlotti beans and winter squash.

- **Cranberries, satsumas, clementines** and **pomegranates**
  are all arriving. There are still plenty of **apples**, **pears** and
  quince.
- **Nuts** are plentiful: **hazelnuts, sweet chestnuts** and **walnuts**
  have all recently ripened.
- Lots of **wild mushrooms** are still around and **white truffles**
  are in season.
- **Duck, goose, grouse, guinea fowl, partridge, pheasant,
  venison** and **wood pigeon** are all in season.
- Winter cheeses such as **Vacherin Mont d'Or** and **Pont-
  l'Évêque** become available, and **Stilton** is at its best.
- **Brill, sardines, skate, clams, mussels** and **oysters** are
  plentiful.

Ingredient of the month – bacon and sausages

Now we eat bacon all year round, but traditionally it was made
in November, for eating through winter. Right up until the end
of the Second World War it was normal for families to keep a
pig in their backyard, or to be a part of a 'pig club' that raised
pigs communally. Pigs would be fed up all year long, and then
killed and their meat cured for storage, with Martinmas, the
12th November, being the traditional date for the first slaughter.
The parts that would spoil quickly were eaten immediately,
others made into brawn and sausages that would keep for a
short time, and the belly and loin made into bacon that would
be ready by Christmas. There are still smallholders that work
with the seasons in this way. Track down those that supply mail
order, as they will often have raised old breeds with greater
amounts of fat and flavour.

FESTIVITIES

Bridgwater carts and Guy Fawkes: the West Country winter carnivals

Some communities mark Guy Fawkes Night with particular gusto, and the towns and villages of Somerset and the West Country are among them. Bridgwater has celebrated Guy Fawkes Night since 1606, but its celebrations have evolved in entirely their own bizarre direction. The West Country winter carnival tradition comprises brightly lit floats known as carts, parading through the chilly night streets to crowds of up to 150,000 in Bridgwater itself, carnival epicentre.

Somerset's historic embrace of Guy Fawkes Night holds clues to the nationwide endurance of this celebration of capture and torture. Crucially, the Gunpowder Plot to blow up the Palace of Westminster and assassinate King James I was a plan by Catholic conspirators in reaction to Catholic persecution. Somerset was staunchly Protestant and anti-Catholic, and had its own Catholic bogeyman in the form of Robert Persons, born at Nether Stowey near Bridgwater. Persons was an influential Jesuit priest involved in attempts to put a Catholic back on the throne. His birthplace's proximity may explain the glee with which the town came to celebrate the failure.

The Observance of 5th November Act was passed in January 1606, a day to celebrate the saving of the life of the king. In that year Bridgwater lit a bonfire, and over the years gangs began using farm carts to bring effigies of the villains to the fire, the ritualised mob lynching with which we are all familiar. This started the tradition of procession which evolved into ever bigger, brighter carts. Now almost no fire is involved and it is not unusual for a cart to cost upwards of £20,000 to create. It may have had a dark start, but the religious origins of the Bridgwater Carnival have been almost forgotten. It is now a chance to see *The Great Gatsby* recreated in light bulbs, complete with high-kicking girls in flapper dresses, with not a hint of anti-Catholic gloating.

N

RECIPES

Cowboy beans

Happily for us, dried beans and smoked meats make perfect partners, the beans soaking up all the meaty, smoky flavour as they gently cook, and bulking out the precious meat. This will feed and warm a Bonfire Night crowd.

Serves 8
Ingredients
400 g dried borlotti beans (or pinto or cannellini beans), soaked overnight
1 onion, chopped
2 tbsp bacon fat or vegetable oil
5 garlic cloves, thinly sliced
1 smoked ham hock
500 ml black coffee
1 bay leaf
1 whole jalapeño chilli
Salt and pepper

Method

Put the beans in a large pot, covered in 2½ cm or so of water, and boil vigorously for 15 minutes. Drain them and reserve the cooking water. In a large, thick-based pot, gently sauté the onion in the fat until it is translucent. Add the garlic and cook for a few more minutes. Add the beans, the ham hock, the black coffee, the bay leaf, the jalapeño chilli and 500 ml of the cooking water, bring to the boil and simmer for up to 3 hours, adding more water if needed, until the beans are soft and the meat is falling away from the bone. Season with salt and pepper and serve in bowls with optional sour cream and grated cheese.

Parkin

Parkin is a traditional oat-based cake of Yorkshire and
Lancashire, always eaten on Bonfire Night. These were areas of
the country where it was too cold and wet to grow wheat, and
so oats were the predominant cereal; hence this is a cake of the
north. It should be made up to a week before it is due to be eaten,
as it only softens and becomes adequately sticky over time.

Makes 16 squares
Ingredients
220 g golden syrup
55 g black treacle
110 g butter
110 g dark brown soft sugar
225 g medium oatmeal
110 g self-raising flour
2 tsp ground ginger
1 tsp mixed ground spice
Pinch of salt
1 large egg, beaten
1 tbsp milk

Method
Grease and line a 20 cm x 20 cm cake tin and preheat the oven
to 140°C/285°F/gas mark 1. If you have electronic scales, place
a small saucepan onto them, set to zero, and weigh in the
golden syrup and black treacle. Add the butter and sugar and
heat gently until all are melted together. Put the oatmeal, flour,
ginger, spice and salt into a large bowl, then stir in the melted
mixture, then the egg and then the milk. Pour into the tin and
bake for around 1½ hours. When it is completely cold, store it
in an airtight tin until Bonfire Night.

N

Diwali sweets

pumpkin keer

CASHEW BARTI

COCONUT LADOO

gulab jamun

jalebi

NATURE

Look out for:
- Larch, beech and oak are among the last trees to colour up and lose their leaves.
- Tits and finches are the birds most likely to be seen in gardens, with occasional glimpses of tree creepers and nuthatches. Rooks and crows begin to dominate in the countryside, along with magpies.
- There are still lots of mushrooms and toadstools appearing in woodlands after damp spells.
- Atlantic salmon have left the sea and are migrating upstream to their place of birth, leaping up any obstacles that get in their way.
- Whooper and Bewick's swans return from the Arctic for the winter.
- Many animals and insects are going into hibernation, or something like it, to see out the winter. Hedgehogs and dormice hibernate. Bats enter a state of reduced metabolism, but emerge on warm days. Ladybirds and peacock butterflies seek out nooks and crannies in sheds and lofts.

N

December

1   Start of meteorological winter

2   First Sunday of Advent

3   First day of Hanukkah (Jewish celebration)

8   Feast of the Immaculate Conception (Christian celebration)

10   Last day of Hanukkah

21   Winter solstice/midwinter

21   Yule (pagan celebration)

21   Start of astronomical winter

24   Christmas Eve

25   Christmas Day

26   Boxing Day

31   New Year's Eve

December takes us full circle, down into the depths of the year and then up and out the other side. The dark triumphs, but briefly. This month there are yet more festivals of light and battles of fire and darkness: Hanukkah, Yule, and the big one, at least in Britain: Christmas. Before it was Christmas Day, the 25th December was celebrated as the birth date of Sol Invictus, the Roman god of the sun, and it is possible that the date was chosen to underline Christ's role as bringer of hope and light. Just as the longest day at midsummer brought a sense of foreboding, the longest night brings with it great optimism. We feast and light fires, lanterns and candles to ward off the dark, and it works. By the end of December the gloomiest days are behind us.

Landscapes and gardens are all bones now, with just little tufts of leaves clinging to the ends of branches, the last produced of the year, determined to have their allotted time. When sunlight comes it is weak and lemony, and the countryside is a watercolour wash of flax, buff and beige, with occasional ink crows and telephone lines. Deep frost shadows can linger for days behind tall hedges and hedgerows, the sun never threatening them. The days may be short and cold but the night is long and beautiful now, with the moon at its highest and clearest, and the stars showing at their brightest. Sometimes it takes darkness to make us appreciate the light, and anyway, you never know what you might see if you step outside on a December night and look up.

THE SKY

Moon phases

New moon – 7th December

1st quarter – 15th December

Full moon – 22nd December

3rd quarter – 29th December

In the night sky this month

3rd	A close approach of the crescent moon with Venus is visible in the pre-dawn sky, above the south-eastern horizon.
13th & 14th	The Geminids meteor shower will produce many meteors, with the radiant 60 degrees above the south-eastern horizon at midnight.
15th	A close approach of the moon and Mars is visible after dusk, and at its highest at 5.45 p.m., 33 degrees above the southern horizon.

The cold winter moon versus the warm summer moon

In winter the northern hemisphere is tilted away from the sun but towards the moon, so the sun is low in the sky but the moon is bright, clear and high. In summer we are tilted towards the sun but away from the moon, so the sun climbs high but the moon stays low (and looks more orange as we view it through a thicker slice of atmosphere). The moon will be at its highest, whitest and brightest this month.

Constellation of the month – Gemini

The constellation of Gemini, the Twins, can be seen low in the east in the early evening, rising high into the sky as the night wears on. It will be right overhead throughout January and February. Find it by drawing an imaginary line down the 'handle' of the Big Dipper and through the 'bowl', then following this line until you reach the twin stars of Pollux and Castor, each representing the starry eye of a twin. In fact they are very different. Pollux is the nearest giant star to the sun, a mere 34 light years off, and Castor is a system of six bluish-white stars and red dwarfs. On a clear, dark night, look just off of the bottom left of the constellation for star cluster M35, visible to the naked eye but quite beautiful through binoculars or a telescope.

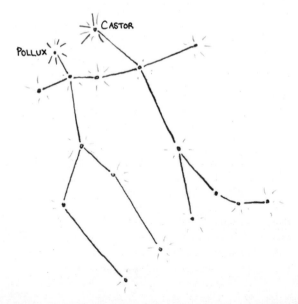

Moon rise and set

	London		Glasgow		
	Rise	Set	Rise	Set	
1st	00.33	14.06	00.22	13.45	
2nd	01.54	14.23	01.39	14.07	
3rd	03.14	14.41	02.54	14.29	
4th	04.33	15.00	04.08	14.53	
5th	05.50	15.21	05.20	15.18	
6th	07.06	15.47	06.31	15.48	
7th	08.17	16.18	07.39	16.23	new moon
8th	09.21	16.57	08.41	17.04	
9th	10.17	17.45	09.35	17.53	
10th	11.02	18.42	10.21	18.47	
11th	11.38	19.44	11.00	19.47	
12th	12.06	20.50	11.32	20.50	
13th	12.28	21.59	11.58	21.54	
14th	12.47	23.08	12.21	22.59	
15th	13.04	–	12.42	–	1st quarter
16th	13.20	00.19	13.02	00.06	
17th	13.36	01.31	13.21	01.14	
18th	13.53	02.46	13.43	02.24	
19th	14.13	04.03	14.07	03.37	
20th	14.38	05.24	14.37	04.52	
21st	15.10	06.46	15.13	06.09	
22nd	15.54	08.05	16.00	07.25	full moon
23rd	16.52	09.15	16.59	08.34	
24th	18.05	10.12	18.10	09.32	
25th	19.27	10.55	19.28	10.19	
26th	20.53	11.28	20.49	10.56	
27th	22.18	11.53	22.09	11.26	
28th	23.42	12.14	23.28	11.52	
29th	–	12.32	–	12.14	3rd quarter
30th	01.02	12.49	00.44	12.36	
31st	02.21	13.07	01.58	12.59	

WEATHER

Although December marks the beginning of meteorological winter, it is not the coldest month. That honour goes to January, mainly because the remnants of summer's warmth that are captured and held in the seas around us ebb away slowly, still having an impact in December. Because of this it is also not, sadly, a month when there is a particularly high chance of snow. In fact, most parts of the country are more likely to see snow at Easter than at Christmas, although this doesn't stop us dreaming. There is a high probability of air frosts though, which have plenty of time to build up over the long dark nights.

Average temperatures (°C):	London 7, Glasgow 4
Average sunshine hours per day:	London 1, Glasgow 1
Average days rainfall:	London 17, Glasgow 22
Average rainfall total (mm):	London 53, Glasgow 120

Day length

During the course of December, day length decreases by:

22 minutes, down to its shortest at 7 hours and 49 minutes on the 21st, and then increases by 5 minutes by the end of the month (London).

28 minutes, down to its shortest at 6 hours 58 minutes on the 21st, and then increases by 7 minutes by the end of the month (Glasgow).

Sunrise and set

| | London | | Glasgow | |
	Rise	Set	Rise	Set
1st	07.44	15.55	08.23	15.49
2nd	07.45	15.54	08.24	15.48
3rd	07.46	15.54	08.26	15.47
4th	07.48	15.53	08.28	15.46
5th	07.49	15.53	08.29	15.46
6th	07.50	15.53	08.31	15.45
7th	07.51	15.52	08.32	15.45
8th	07.53	15.52	08.33	15.44
9th	07.54	15.52	08.35	15.44
10th	07.55	15.52	08.36	15.43
11th	07.56	15.51	08.37	15.43
12th	07.57	15.51	08.38	15.43
13th	07.58	15.51	08.39	15.43
14th	07.59	15.51	08.40	15.43
15th	08.00	15.52	08.41	15.43
16th	08.00	15.52	08.42	15.43
17th	08.01	15.52	08.43	15.43
18th	08.02	15.52	08.44	15.43
19th	08.03	15.53	08.44	15.44
20th	08.03	15.53	08.45	15.44
21st	08.04	15.53	08.46	15.44
22nd	08.04	15.54	08.46	15.45
23rd	08.05	15.54	08.47	15.46
24th	08.05	15.55	08.47	15.46
25th	08.05	15.56	08.47	15.47
26th	08.06	15.56	08.47	15.48
27th	08.06	15.57	08.48	15.49
28th	08.06	15.58	08.48	15.49
29th	08.06	15.59	08.48	15.50
30th	08.06	16.00	08.48	15.51
31st	08.06	16.01	08.48	15.53

THE SEA

Average sea temperature

Orkney:	9.1°C
Scarborough:	8.8°C
Blackpool:	9.4°C
Brighton:	12°C
Penzance:	11.7°C

Spring and neap tides

The spring tide is the most extreme tide of the month, with the highest rises and falls, and the neap tide is the least extreme, with the smallest. Exact timings vary around the coast, but expect each around the following dates:

Spring tides:	8th–9th and 23rd–24th
Neap tides:	1st–2nd, 16th–17th and 30th–31st

Drift seeds

December is a fine month for interesting flotsam, so walk along the tide line on a west-coast beach – especially just after storms or the highest tides of the month around the 8th and the 23rd – and see what you can find. Atlantic currents circulate in a clockwise direction, and in early winter anything floating on these currents is given a helping hand by westerly gales, sometimes the tail ends of West Indian hurricanes. Exotic seeds that fall into the sea in the Caribbean can bob and float along on these currents and wash up on our shores.

In Ireland sea beans (*Mucuna sloanei* seeds), sea hearts (*Entada gigas*) and Mary's beans (*Lathyrus japonicus subsp. maritimus*) have long been considered lucky finds with protective qualities, and hung in cattle byres and around children's necks.

Drift seeds

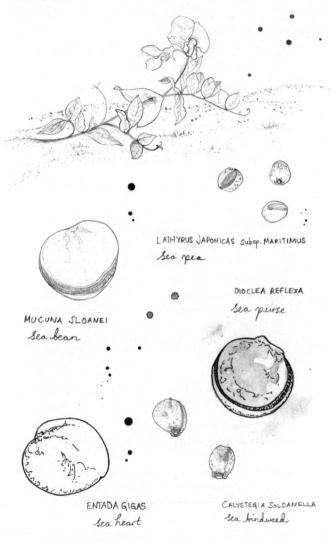

LATHYRUS JAPONICAS subsp. MARITIMUS
Sea pea

DIOCLEA REFLEXA
Sea purse

MUCUNA SLOANEI
Sea bean

ENTADA GIGAS
Sea heart

CALYSTEGIA SOLDANELLA
Sea bindweed

THE GARDEN

Planting by the moon

3rd quarter to new moon: 1st–7th. Prune. Harvest for storage. Fertilise and mulch the soil.

New moon to 1st quarter: 7th–15th. Sow crops that develop below ground. Dig the soil.

1st quarter to full moon: 15th–22nd. Sow crops that develop above ground. Plant seedlings and young plants.

Full moon to 3rd quarter: 22nd–29th. Harvest crops for immediate eating. Harvest fruit.

Jobs in the garden

- Check and improve wires, ties and stakes on trees and climbers before high winds. Hold everything firmly in place so nothing gets bashed about.
- Plant new bare-root top fruit and soft fruit now for fruit next summer and autumn. This is prime time for buying and planting apples, pears, quinces, raspberries, blackberries, gooseberries, blackcurrants and redcurrants.
- Make a bean trench in which to plant next year's beans. The trench should be as long as you want your row to be and about a foot deep and wide. Line it with newspaper and fill it with kitchen waste as you have it, topping with soil each time. This will provide a rich root run for these greedy and thirsty plants.

Glut of the month – Brussels sprouts

Sprouts are at their sweetest and most flavourful after a frost. Harvest from the bottom of the stalk upwards, as those sprouts at the base 'blow' and lose their shape first.

- Make a nutty winter coleslaw by mixing shredded Brussels sprouts with grated carrot, apple, toasted walnuts and mayonnaise.

- Cold, cooked sprouts come back to life when fried in butter until the edges are crisped, or as a part of a bubble and squeak, with a runny fried egg on top.
- Sprout tops are another gardener's perk: loose leafy bunches, sometimes with baby sprouts attached. Harvesting them now will have no impact on the rest of the crop, so chop them off and fry them up with crispy bacon and sage.

Garden task – plant a shrub for winter fragrance

This would seem like a crazy time to flower, and with so few pollinators about, most of the garden packed up long ago, saving its flowering energies for a time when success with the birds and the butterflies appears more likely. But every niche in nature will be filled, and there are some plants that flower now precisely because there is so little competition. Because of the winter paucity of pollinators, these outliers do not rely on the visual extravaganzas most flowers employ – for a bee to be attracted by the sight of a flower it needs to be buzzing pretty close by, and the chances right now are slim. Instead, winter-flowering plants produce huge volumes of fragrance, from tiny petalled flowers, all the better to withstand winter's vagaries. On a mild winter day the clean, citric fragrance of a witch hazel or the wafting spiciness of a daphne will carry far further than its immediate surroundings, signalling to anything in the vicinity that there is pollen to be had, if they just take the time to search it out. This is good news for the gardener, as is the fact that this is shrub-planting time. Track down a winter-flowering shrub and get it into the ground now, and you will forever more be able to pick little sprigs that will fill your house with fragrance in mid-winter. Witch hazel and daphne are the two most commonly grown, but look also for little and evergreen *Sarcococca confusa*, with its huge tangy orange scent; sweet-scented *Viburnum x bodnantense*, 'Dawn'; and the aptly named wintersweet (*Chimomanthus praecox*).

D

KITCHEN

In season

- Jerusalem artichokes, carrots, beetroot, leeks, parsnips, cauliflower, Brussels sprouts, kale, winter cabbage, and stored potatoes, borlotti beans and winter squash.
- Cranberries, satsumas, clementines and pomegranates are arriving from southern Europe and the US. There are still plenty of home-grown apples, pears and quince.
- Nuts are plentiful: hazelnuts, sweet chestnuts and walnuts.
- Black truffles are in season.
- Ask specialist butchers for duck, goose, grouse, guinea fowl, partridge, pheasant, venison and wood pigeon. There is – fairly obviously – lots of turkey to be had.
- Vacherin cheeses, only made in autumn and winter, are available now from Switzerland and France. This is also the season for Stilton, extra-mature artisan cheddars, Chevrotin des Aravis, Comté, Époisses and Gruyère.
- Brill, sardines, skate, clams, mussels and oysters.

Ingredient of the month – Stilton and Stichelton

Stilton has long been considered a cheese to be eaten at Christmas, creamy and strong and perfectly offset by a small glass of port and a crackling fire. This is because it used to take between six and eight months to mature, so cheese made from April to June would be ready in December. Now maturing times have shortened, Stilton changes in character through the year: the first batch made with spring milk has a fresher flavour; the Christmas batch is sweeter. It has protected status and can only be made with pasteurised milk in Derbyshire, Leicestershire and Nottinghamshire, by a strictly controlled method (cheese made in Stilton itself, the Cambridgeshire village the cheese is named after, cannot be called Stilton). Stichelton is made in Nottinghamshire by the same method as Stilton but with unpasteurised milk and the original Stilton starter culture, not used in official Stilton manufacture since 1989. Stichelton may be the original name of the village of Stilton, just as this may be closer to the original Stilton recipe.

FESTIVITIES

Midwinter evergreens

The plants that we now associate with Christmas, that we use to deck our halls and to stand and giggle underneath, are remnants of an older celebration of the longest night and the shortest day: Yule, the winter solstice, midwinter. Midwinter celebrations were bountiful, fire-filled and optimistic, announcing the returning of the light. Although it does not feel like it now, from here on the days begin to get incrementally longer, and that is a thing that feels worth celebrating even in these days of 24-hour corner shops. It must have felt like a lifeline being thrown then.

Evergreens symbolised life at a time when most plants have dropped their leaves and all around looks dead, and so they became integral to this festival of continuity and reassurance. Berries represented fertility, and so were also revered at this most barren of moments. Holly was thought a female plant and mistletoe male, and they were often hung together, hence the kissing. Christmas wreaths themselves are also extremely ancient, dating back at least to Roman times when they decorated homes during Saturnalia, the Roman festival of midwinter. The wreath is thought to be symbolic of the wheel of the year (the word 'yule' may come from the Nordic word for wheel, *houl*), and acts as another reminder that this is a pivotal moment and that this darkness and cold will pass. Hang this heartening wheel of evergreens on your door to welcome guests, then eat and drink and celebrate the hope and promise that these dark days bring.

D

RECIPES

Quince and hazelnut mincemeat

You can use this straight away, but the earlier you make it the better, and it will of course keep for years. Quince is hard and astringent when raw, only turning coral-hued and yieldingly sweet and aromatic when slowly cooked, making this recipe slightly fussier than most. If you don't have the time or the inclination (or the quinces), you can make this with raw apples, but the quince is worth the trouble.

Makes 6–8 jars
Ingredients
To poach the quince
Pared zest and juice of 1 lemon
1 l water
1 kg quince
1 piece star anise
1 vanilla pod
5 tbsp honey

For the mincemeat
400 g currants
400 g sultanas
400 g seedless raisins
200 g blanched, toasted hazelnuts, roughly chopped
100 g chopped candied peel
225 g soft brown sugar
½ tsp freshly grated nutmeg
½ tsp ground cloves

1 tsp ground cinnamon
½ tsp allspice
Juice and zest of 1 lemon
250 g shredded suet
200 ml apple brandy/cognac

Method

To poach the quince, first put the lemon juice and lemon zest into the water in a large saucepan. Use a vegetable peeler to remove the skin of the quince, then quarter it with a sturdy knife and remove the core and any bruised or damaged bits. Drop the pieces into the liquid as you work. Add the rest of the poaching ingredients and bring to the boil, then simmer for about an hour, until the quince has turned pink. Leave to cool completely, then dice the quince, not too fine (do not throw away the cooking liquid as it makes a beautiful syrup for champagne cocktails or pouring over ice cream).

In a large bowl combine the quince with the rest of the ingredients. Stir, cover and leave to sit for a few hours. Stir again and pack into sterilised jars and seal.

D

Roasting chestnuts (properly)

Chestnuts roasted on an open fire should be soft and yielding, the struggle to crack them open rewarded by the steaming innards: nuttiness combining with comforting carbohydrate, all tinged with a sweet smokiness. In reality they are often burned on one side and raw on the other, and you have put your poor thumbs through some amount of pain and scorching for nothing but disappointment. It is less romantic, but they cook far better in an oven, and can then be finished off over the fire for a bit of characterful charring if you like. Preheat your oven to 200°C/390°F/gas mark 6. Check over your chestnuts and throw away any that have holes in them, then lay each flat side down and cut a cross right through the skin on its back. Wash them well (this allows a little water in, which helps separate skin from nut), and put them into a baking tray to roast for about 30 minutes, shaking to turn them half way through. (If you must cook over the fire, do so over low embers for at least this length of time, and shake frequently to move them around.) Crack open the skins while they are still hot, and eat smeared with cold butter and sprinkled with salt.

NATURE

Look out for:

- Both male and female robins are singing. By mid-January they will have paired up with a mate and the females will fall quiet.
- Tawny owls are also marking out territory, and can be heard in woodlands making the distinctive 'two-wit' and 'two-woo' calls.
- Holly berries are at their most ripe and beautiful if they have not been eaten by the birds yet. Ivy is flowering and providing pollen for the few bees that are around. Look out for bunches of mistletoe, now easily seen high in the branches of bare apple and lime trees.
- Teasel heads are all dried out now and are looking sculptural in road verges. They are also a perfect source of food for goldfinches, which can reach the seeds within with their slender beaks.
- Estuaries are full of waders all winter, providing a reliable source of food and never freezing because of the sea. Kingfishers and otters move to estuaries now for the same reasons.
- Foxes do not hibernate and may be seen more frequently in cities as leaner food sources lead to boldness.

Murmurations

This month breathtaking murmurations reach their peak. Murmurations are the gatherings and swooping of thousands of starlings on winter evenings above reed beds. They begin to amass in November, but reach their greatest numbers this month and next, with up to 100,000 birds in some flocks. In the early evening, just before dusk, the birds take to the sky in such masses that the sky is blackened. They then move in seemingly coordinated swirls and swoops until the sky is dark, when they settle down to roost for the night. It may be a way of fending off predators or of keeping warm on the cold nights.

ACKNOWLEDGEMENTS

Thank you to all of those who supported and championed this book through the strange and wonderful process of crowdfunding. It was a brilliant and exhausting thing, and your encouragement warmed my heart and made this possible. Some people were particularly helpful in cheerleading and in offering help to create crowdfunding rewards, and I would like to particularly thank India Knight, Sara Venn, Mark Diacono, Arne Maynard, Emma Bradshaw, Claire Thomson, Genevieve Taylor, Danielle Coombes, and my mum, Cath Read, in this regard.

Working with Unbound has been a joy and I would like to thank Philip Connor for initial enthusiasm and guiding the book through the early stages, and DeAndra Lupu for picking up the baton and guiding the book to completion with such energy. Thank you to Miranda Ward and Kate Quarry for meticulous copy editing and proofreading. Emma Dibben's illustrations are magical and have proved perfect for the almanac, as I knew they would be. I was determined to have the brilliant Matt Cox of Newman+Eastwood as designer as I knew he would wrestle the many strands of disparate information into something elegant and beautiful, and he has done precisely that. Thank you.

I have had to reach out for help in compiling much of the information contained here. Thank you to my dad, Jack Leendertz, for his amazing work on the 'Sky at night' sections, without which I would still be puzzling over tables and graphs. Thanks also to Steve Byford for excellent and helpful astronomical thoughts, to Kate Head for tidal guidance, and to Peter Gibbs for advice on all things meteorological. I am delighted to be including recipes from Ishita DasGupta to mark Holi, Nisrin Abuorf for Ramadan, and Natasha Miles for Notting Hill Carnival. Thank you all for your expertise and enthusiasm, and for providing such perfect recipes for these moments in the year.

I have also depended upon various sources of information, many of which are worth visiting or tracking down yourself if this almanac has piqued your interest. Thank you to Time and Date (www.timeanddate.com) for their generous permission to make use of some of their many tables of information. Their website is a really fabulous resource. I would also like to acknowledge and point readers towards a number of books that helped me along the way, including: *Moon Gardening* by John Harris; *The English Year* by Steve Roud; *Philip's Month-by-Month Star Finder* by John Woodruff and Wil Tirion; *The Wrong Kind of Snow: The complete daily companion to the British Weather* by Antony Woodward and Robert Penn; *Seasonal Food* by Paul Waddington; *Allotment Month by Month* by Alan Buckingham; *Sea Beans and Nickar Nuts* by E. Charles Nelson; and *The Complete Guide to British Wildlife* by N. Arlott, R. Fitter and A. Fitter. The websites seatemperature.org, holiday-weather.com and plantmaps.com are also good sources of information. I can also highly recommend the Star Walk app for keeping track of the stars and planets mentioned herein. It is great fun and quite addictive.

Thank you to my gorgeous family, Michael, Rowan and Meg, for your support, encouragement and (increasingly, Meg!) input.

ABOUT THE AUTHOR

Lia Leendertz is an award-winning garden and food writer.
She writes a weekly column for the *Telegraph*, a monthly
column for *The Garden* magazine and a long-running
series on growing and eating seasonally for *Simple Things*
magazine. She also contributes frequently to the *Guardian*
and *Gardens Illustrated*. She is the author of several gardening
books and the cookbook *Petal, Leaf, Seed: Cooking with the
Garden's Treasures*.

ABOUT THE ILLUSTRATOR

Emma Dibben is an illustrator living and working in Bristol.
Her work is internationally acclaimed and features in books
and magazines around the globe. Emma's illustrations are
inspired by the great loves of her life, gardening and food –
she can often be found drawing in her allotment. View more
of her work at: www.emmadibben.com

INDEX

SUPPORTERS

Unbound is a new kind of publishing house. Our books are funded directly by readers. This was a very popular idea during the late eighteenth and early nineteenth centuries. Now we have revived it for the internet age. It allows authors to write the books they really want to write and readers to support the books they would most like to see published.

The names listed below are of readers who have pledged their support and made this book happen. If you'd like to join them, visit www.unbound.com.

A

Mark Abbott-Compton
Jessica Adams
Maureen Adams
David Akroyd
Lynne Elizabeth Alexander
James Alexander-Sinclair
Anji Allen
Marian Allen
Louise Santa Ana
Jill Anderson
Liz Anderson
Melody Angell
Michelle Armitage
Richard Ashcroft
Amelia Ashton
Jo Atkins

B

K B
Michael Baines
Karen Ball
Nicola Bannock
Clare Barnett

Joanna Baron
Laurie Barrett
Helen Bates
Susannah Batstone
Sarah Bayley
Jane Beck
Fiona Beckett
Adrian Belcher
Abigail Bell
Lucy Bellamy
Kathy Bellis
Ronnie Bendall
Emli Bendixen
Chris Bennell
Rhiannon Benson
Benny Louise Bernard
Jude Bevan
Anne Beyer
Ali Bienemann
Deborah Bird
Lindsay Birt
Christian Bishop
Charlotte Bland
Sar Bleary

Mary Borders
Marian Boswall
Hartley Botanic
Kate Bradbury
Paul Bradley
Emma Bradshaw
Jane Brant
Janice Bridger
Louisa Thomsen Brits
Tess Broad
Katherine Broomfield
Nicky Brown
Sinead Browning
Isabel Bryony
Paul Bullivant
Andrea Burden
Sandy Burnfield
Ali Burns
Bernadette Bustin
Annone Butler
Caroline Butler
Laura Butler
Heather Butt
Maggie Butt
Lisa Byford

C

T C
Serena Calderisi
Sean James Cameron
(seanjcameron.com)
Alison Campbell
Rick Challener
Jenny Chandler
John Luke Chapman
Michelle Chapman
Kate Charlton
Peter Charnley

Georgina Churchlow
Sarah Clapham
Jane Clare
John Clark
Kate Clark
Martin Clarke
Pete Clasby
Xanthe Clay
Martyn Clayton
Lucy Clements
Lizzie Clulee
Gina Collia
Emily Comyn
Patricia Concannon
Jane Conway
Jess Cook
Philip Coombes
Danielle Coombs
Ellie Cornell
Angharad Corona
Ana Corral
Charlotte Mendes Costa
Ann Cowie
Alan Cowley
Sarah Cowper
Chris Cox
Lee Cox
Laura Cramer
George Crawford
Oliver Crawford
Jennifer Crowe
Sarah Crowson
Julia Croyden
Hazel Culley
Harriet Cunningham
Louise Curley
Morag Currie
Elly Curshen

Julie Curtis
Robin Curtis
Tim Curtis

D

Francesca D'Alessandro
Tammi Dallaston
Fleur Darkin
Ishita DasGupta
Deborah Davies
Harriet Fear Davies
Justine Dawson
Rachel de Thame
Jane Delaney
Philippe Demeur
Amber Dennis
Julie Denton
Lindsay Derbyshire
Jessica Derricourt
Carole Diacono
Mark Diacono
Emma Dibben
Ian Dickson
Sharon Digweed
Sheila Dillon
Lorna Doherty
Sally Doherty
Julie Dolphin
Donata
Peter Donegan
Polly Donnellan
Eleanor Driscoll
Mary-Anne Driscoll
Wendy Duddy
David Duffy
Tim Duller
Claire Dunnage

E

Dave Eagle
Thom Eagle
Tom Eaglestone
Alexandra Earl
Joanna Eden
Kelly Emery
Suze Emmett
Melodie Escott
Clare Esson
Cath Evans

F

Jacki Fahy
Sally Falconer
Amanda Fallan
Joan Fawcett
Charlotte Featherstone
Jacqui Ferguson
Lynne Fernandes
Kathryn Flegg
Lizzy Fone
Adriana Ford
Elaina Ford
Joanna Fortnam
Susanne Frank
Gillian French
Sonja Froebel

G

Jo Gadsden
Paul Gaffikin
Victoria Gaiger
Rachael Garden
Vergette Gardens
Vincent Gauci
Rose George
Georgina & Isi

Peter Gibbs
Hannah Gibson
Jo Gibson
Trish Gibson
Charlotte Gilbey
Blake Gilchrist
Cherry Gilchrist
Chris Gilchrist
Louisa Gilhooly
Karen Gimson
Alfred Gliddon
Nick Glydon
Lucy Glynn
Helen Goddard
Diane Godfrey
Lis Golding
Charlotte Goldney
Sophie Goldsworthy
Imogen Gowar
Joanne Grace
Emma Grainger
Jo Gray
Karen Gray
Helen Green
Jo Green
Sandy Grimes
Hampstead Guesthouse
Elaine Guilding
Annie Guilfoyle
Sandie Guine

H

Stephen J Hackett
Nicola Haggett
Dorothy Halfhide
Lucy Hall
Neil Hall
Mark Hammond
Catherine Hamp

Anita Hannam
Celia Hart
Caitlin Harvey
Donna Harvey
James Peter Robinson Harvey
Jez Hastings
Kate Head
Abby Healey
Andrew Hearse
Emma Heasman-Hunt
Anthony Heath
Nina Hedderick-Reid
Anna Herbert
Dawn Heuff
Benedict Hewston
Clare Heyting
Anna Higgins
Alice Hilaire
Julia Hodgson
Ulrich Hoffmann
Sophie Holborow
Bridget Holding
Ruth Holland
Richard Holliman
Sara Holman
Richard Hood
Catherine Hookway
Nicola Hope
Claire Hopley
Sebastian Horlitz
Teresa Horn
Catherine Horwood
Julia Howell
Ellen Hughes
Jill Hunt
Ray Hunter
Kim Hurst
Kate Hutchings

I

Edward Ikin
Judith Illsley
Jason Ingram
Tim Ingram
Ingreedies
Dawn Isaac

J

Paul Jabore
Victoria Jack
Christine Jackson
Dawn Jackson
Michelle Jago
Miranda Janatka
Caroline Jennings
Catherine Jolliffe
Melissa Jolly
Charlie Jones
Dorothy Jones
Roz Jones
Siân Jones
Vicki Jordan
Jennifer Joy-Matthews

K

Miriam kelly
Christina Kennedy
Marion Keogh
Mobeena Khan
Dan Kieran
Fi Kirkpatrick
Lorna Knapman
Afsaneh Knight
India Knight
Anna Koska

L

Lesley Labram
Samantha Lacey
Gillian Lamprell
Phoebe Lamprell
Joe Lang
Valerie Langfield
Paul Ban Lavery
Chantal Laws
Alison Layland
Corinne Layton
Nikki Leader
Jack Leendertz
Anna Leendertz-Ford
Maryline Leese
Stephanie Leijnse
Marc Leverton
Alison Levey
Annie Levy
Jamie Lewis
Penny Lewis
Ryan Lewis
Claire Lindow
Caroline Lister
Sue Llewellyn
Ali Lloyd-Jones
Elspeth Loades
Matt Locke
Charlotte Lorimer
Tamar Lucas
Liz Luckwell
Kathryn Lwin

M

Lesley Mackley
Katie Maddock
Jessica Magill
Clarrie Maguire

Maddy Maine
Laetitia Maklouf
Donna Malcolm
Nick Mann
Helen Marini
Emma Marriott
Madeleine Marshall
Ian Martin
Lisa Martin
Melanie Martin
Jennifer Mason
Evie Matthew
Claire Maycock
Grace Maycock
Arne Maynard
Anne McAllister
Karen McCann
Liza McCarron
Katie McClymont
Karen McElligott
Sophie McGrath
Ella Mcs
Grace Mears
Petra Hoyer Millar
Hannah Miller
Jennifer Mills
Elaine Mitchell
John Mitchinson
Colin Moat
Adam Moliver
Alison Morgan
Diana Morgan
Chris Mosler
Ben Mountfield
Jane Myburgh

N

Linda Nathan
Carlo Navato
Gaynor Newnham
Sally Nex
Sophie Nioche
Luane Nisbet
Sabra Noordeen
Carol Norton
Maria Nunn
Patricia Nunn
Scarlett Nunn

O

Andrew O'Brien
Penn O'Gara
Sarah Oates
Mark Oliff
Emma Olver
Paul Oppe
Linzy Outtrim
Amy Overy
Nia Owen-Cortez

P

Nicky Parkinson
Laura Pashby
Milly Patrzalek
Billy Paul
Matthew Payne
Chris Pearce
Faye Peel
Miranda Pender
Jane Perrone
Charlotte Petts
Jill Phillips
Kathy Phillips
Catherine Phipps

Catherine Pickersgill
Jane Pike
Wendy Pillar
Neal & Kerry Whitehouse Piper
Jean Pollard
Justin Pollard
Alison Pollock
Justine Poole
Beki Pope
Anna Portch
Julieanne Porter
Gwen Potter
Ann-Marie Powell
Janet Pretty
Linda Proud
Ann Pugh
Anna Pugh
Lorraine Pullen
Janet Purdie
Lucy Purdy

R

Nicola Ramsden
Beryl Randall
Lyssa Randolph
Benjamin Ranyard
Carol Rasberry
Daniel Rawling
Cath Read
Sam Read
Helen Obee Reardon
Sue Reekie
Sam Richards
Andrew Riddell
Maddi Riddell
Robyn Riddoch
Liz Ridgway

James Robbins
Ann Roberts
Diane Roberts
John Roberts
Juliet Roberts
Pamela Roberts
Pearl Roberts
Sarah Roberts
Debora Robertson
Catherine Rossi

S

Susan Roughton
Charlie Rowlands
Amanda Russell
Harriet Rycroft
June Saddington – TheCynicalGardener
Takako Saito
Tim Saltmarsh
Sarah Salway
Tommy Samuel
Jenny Sanderson
Melanie Savage
Marinda Schoeman
Kate Scott
Louise Scruton-Evans
Katie Seaman
Barbara Segall
Heather Shann
Jennifer Shannon
Jane Sharp
Candy & Brian Simpson
Desmond Simpson
Maria Simpson
Michael Simpson
Sandra Simpson
Belinda Simson

Helen Skuse
Naomi Slade
Nigel Slater
Drew Smith
Rebecca Smith
Sharon Julie Smith
Gaby Solly
Mog Solstice
Jennie Spears
Andrew Spencer
Delyth Spikes
Claire Spiller
Sara Spratt
Annie Stanford
Peter Stephenson
Rebecca Stone
Helen Sumbler
Vikki Summers
Claire Sumner
Simon Suter
Josh Sutton
Rachel Swingewood

T

Barbara Taylor
Genevieve Taylor
Archie & Hannah Thomas
Craig Thompson
Helen Thompson
Jo Thompson
Claire Thomson
Sarah Togher
Solitaire Townsend
Emma Townshend
Neill Trebble
Jeff Tupholme
Susie Turner
Jeanette Turner-King

Curzon Tussaud
James Tutt
Alice Tyler
Sue Tyler
Trish Tyler

U

Miss Understood

V

Tilly Vacher
Anneke van Eijkern
Annemarie van Ommen
Deborah Vass
Janet Vaughan
Hannah Velten
Sara Venn
Beki Vince
Gea Visser

W

John Walker
Peter Walker
Peter Walker
Midge Walling
Jack Wallington
Helen Walsh
Julia Walter
Karen Walton
Judith Warbey
Debbie Ward
Rachel Wareing
Rachel Warne
Rebekka Warnes-Studd
Holly Watkins
Tamsin Westhorpe
Michaela White
Annalise Whittaker

Christine Wild
Hollie Newton Wilkes
Gordon Wilkie
Jeff Willans
Beth Williams
Julie Williams
Si Williams
Dick Willis
Jane Willis
Nic Wilson
Clive Witcomb
Georgina Wolfe
James K Wood
Elizabeth Woodhead
Rebecca Woods
Rory Woodward
Peter Wrapson
Vicky Wyer

Y
Chris Young
Julie Young
Kirstie Young